ALPHABET SOUP

LINDA KILGANNON

Grosvenor House
Publishing Limited

This book is published by
Grosvenor House Publishing Ltd
Link House
140 The Broadway, Tolworth, Surrey, KT6 7HT.
www.grosvenorhousepublishing.co.uk

A CIP record for this book
is available from the British Library

ISBN 978-1-80381-993-8

DEDICATION

I dedicate this book to my children, Colin, Matthew and Christopher, to their wives Moira, Tracey and Katy and to my grandchildren Lily, Jago, Lealand, Dylan, Emily and Samuel.

I thank God for the gift of such a wonderful family, for the joy they bring and for the treasured memories I have and will continue to have.

I love you all.

'Children are a gift from the Lord.' (*New Living Translation*)

PREFACE

This book has evolved over a small number of years as the Lord first gave me the title and then inspired me with a word for each letter of the alphabet. Specific Bible verses, to be used as a key verse or verses to head each chapter led me down a particular route for study as I focused on how to use the text of the book to help nourish our spiritual well-being.

It is not my intention that the reader should treat this book as something to be read sequentially from start to finish. Rather, I would prefer the reader to turn to the Contents page and allow the Holy Spirit to prompt and guide them to a particular theme, as each theme is based on a specific Biblical verse or verses*. This may mean some repetition over time, or some passages not being read at all. If that is God's will, so be it.

I pray this book may move you to look deeper into your own spiritual health.

* Unless otherwise stated all Bible references are taken from the New International Version Bible.

CONTENTS

ABIDE

Key verse: John 15:4. (KJV) "Abide in me and I in you."

In a biblical context abide means to remain or stay and more modern translations use remain and stay in their translations of this verse of John's Gospel. However, I feel the word abide has more depth to it and presents a sense of intimacy as well as safety and security. It is interesting to note that the letter 'i' is in the middle of the word as if it is being shielded by the two letters either side of it.

Chapter 15 of John's Gospel begins by using the metaphor of the vine to identify the role of the Father (the gardener), of Jesus (the vine) and the disciples or followers (the branches), who are committed to following Jesus. The role of the Father is to look after his garden, tending all the different plants, each having their own special requirements. Here, as the 'vinedresser' his role is to tend the vine, cutting out the branches that do not bear fruit (those that do not abide in Jesus) and pruning the branches that are bearing fruit (those that do abide in Jesus) in order that they may become more fruitful.

So what does it mean to 'abide' in Him? The branch is permanently attached to the vine unless it has been cut off and discarded as being fruitless, or pruned so that it may become more fruitful. Being attached to the vine allows the disciple to be in a permanent relationship with Jesus, for without Jesus in our lives we are powerless and fruitless. In John 15:5 Jesus proclaims, "Without me you can do nothing." Life comes to the branches from the vine. Life comes to the believer through the words of Jesus who says when praying for himself, "Your word is truth." (*John 17:17*) Jesus, as the 'True Vine' provides all the nourishment that the branch needs. And, it is a two-way street as Jesus demonstrated in his relationship with the disciples. He was committed to them, supporting and guiding them on their journey and occasionally rebuking them. But abiding goes beyond just a personal relationship and desire to do what pleases our Lord. It requires us to submit every area of our life – intellectual, emotional, financial and social to the scrutiny of the gardener. We have to bring every thought, every action, every word we speak into 'captivity' to the obedience of Christ, "We take captive every thought to make it obedient to Christ." (*2 Corinthians 10:5*)

What then, is the purpose of 'abiding' in Jesus? Fellowship and intimacy are a natural outcome of abiding in Jesus, but the main purpose of abiding in Jesus is to bear fruit, or as indicated in John 15:8, 'much fruit'. In order to produce this fruit we need to get nourishment from the vine. As Christians, we receive this nourishment through His word and then demonstrate the fruit of that nourishment through our life and ministry. The fruit is then observed by those around us, be it family, friends, colleagues, neighbours or casual acquaintances. By our words and actions, these people can gain a picture of who Jesus is and the impact and benefits of believing in Him can bring. In Jesus' own words we are, "Showing yourselves to be my disciples." (*John 15:8*)

How do we abide in Him? Having accepted Jesus into our lives as our Saviour we need to be filled with the Holy Spirit. The Holy Spirit, or 'helper', as Jesus termed Him will guide us and help us to develop an intimate and personal relationship with Jesus as we listen and pay attention to the 'still small voice' of the Holy Spirit.

Read His word and be obedient to His commands. Jesus says, in verse 9 of John, Chapter 15, "If you obey my commands

ABIDE

you will remain (abide) in my love." We can ask the Holy Spirit
to enlighten us as we read the word, to amplify for us in what
areas of our life we need to respond. Then, through prayer to
address these areas and to develop within us a true desire to do
God's will in our lives. Abiding in Jesus enables us to pray with
confidence and boldness and then to experience answers to
our prayers. Jesus goes on to say, in the same verse, that he has
obeyed his Father's commands and so remains (abides) in His
love and he tells the disciples this so that His joy may be in us
and that our joy may be complete.

Be dependent on Him. It is so easy to do everything in
our own strength and fail to recognise that there is a superior
force at work. It is also easy to hand our problems to Jesus
and then take them back almost immediately when nothing
seems to change. To give our concerns, anxieties and problems
to Jesus, especially when these are personal and sometimes
the cause of great hurt takes courage, but the benefits are
enormous.

There are consequences to abiding in Him and bearing fruit.
The most important of these is that we glorify our Father as we
exhibit the love of God to others. This is the only motive and
aim we should have.

Secondly, we become linked in to the unity and love shared
by the Father and the Son. Jesus says, "As the Father has loved
me, so have I loved you." (John 15:9) The son's love to the
disciples and on to us, was grounded on the Father's love for
him. The pattern of their love and the subsequent obedience of
Jesus, rests entirely on the relationship between the father and
the son. As a child of God we can tap into that unique
relationship.

Thirdly, if we continue to abide in Jesus and are obedient to
His word then Jesus says in John 15 and verse 7, "Ask whatever
you wish and it will be given to you," What a promise.

So, where next? We can all recognise that in today's world our lives are complex and often complicated, whether by personal experiences, circumstances or relationships. However, there is no condition or experience in life where we cannot abide in Him and draw strength and comfort from whatever we are experiencing. The hymn 'Abide with me', which at one time was always sung before the start of the FA Cup Final has words which reflect that when all else around is falling apart we will still triumph if we abide in the Lord.

Abide with me; fast falls the eventide,
The darkness deepens; Lord, with me abide;
When other helpers fail and comforts flee.
Help of the helpless, oh, abide with me.

Swift to its close ebbs out life's little day;
Earth's joys grow dim, its glories pass away;
Change and decay in all around I see–
O Thou who changest not, abide with me.

I fear no foe, with Thee at hand to bless;
Ills have no weight; and tears no bitterness;
Where is death's sting?
Where, grave, thy victory?
I triumph still, if Thou abide with me.

Hold Thou Thy cross before my closing eyes;
Shine through the gloom and point me to the skies;
Heav'n's morning breaks and earth's vain shadows flee;

In life, in death, O Lord, abide with me

Abide with me, abide with me.   *Henry Francis Lyte*

The Lord is our place of safety and security.

The question then becomes – are we about the Father's business and abiding in His house, or do we only pop in when we need something?

BELIEVE

Key verses: Romans 10:9–10. "If you confess with your mouth, Jesus is Lord and believe in your heart that God raised him from the dead, you will be saved. For it is with your heart that you believe and are justified and it is with your mouth that you confess that you are saved."

To believe is to accept that something is true, especially without proof. *Nelson's Bible Dictionary* states that, 'A person who believes is one who takes God at His word and trusts in him for salvation.' The word belief in Greek is pistis, which translates as confidence or trust.

The word believe is in such common currency today that it can easily lead to misunderstanding. To some, to believe means nothing more than an expression of what they expect to happen or hope to achieve: 'I believe I can be in time to pick up the children from school.' To others, to believe is to hold a certain perspective or opinion: 'I believe that Seve Ballesteros was the greatest ever golfer.' To yet others, to believe is to agree intellectually with a set of historical facts such as, Jesus being the son of God who spent time on earth in human form and who performed miracles. But, accepting these as historical facts is not enough. They must be accepted, internalised and taken as true. There is no sense in which the person believing in historical facts has moved to a position where they are trusting in Jesus for their salvation, which is what the biblical definition of believe conveys. As one of our key verses details, the response has to move from the head to the heart.

Salvation means that we have been saved from and rescued from sin and death. We are asking here that a man believes in the resurrection of Christ. The resurrection is the focal point of everything in the life and ministry of Christ. Once you believe everything else falls into place – the incarnation, His life, the miracles, His ascension and returning. The reality is that God raised Jesus from the dead. If you say, 'I believe in his resurrection and that God raised him up,' then Jesus has accomplished what God wanted. The atonement of the sins of the world.

Paul says in Romans 10:9, that to believe in your heart that God raised Jesus from the dead means that you will be saved. He means that in so believing you affirm the deity of Christ and the death and atonement of Christ. Not only the resurrection of Christ, His ascension, His priestly work and His coming glory. Everything revolves around the resurrection.

John Chapter 1 verse 12 reads, "Yet to all who received him, to those who believe in his name, he gave the right to become children of God – children born not of natural descent, nor human decision or a husband's will, but born of God." Membership of God's family is by grace alone – the gift of God, never by human achievement.

In John 3:14,15, we read, "Just as Moses lifted up the snake in the desert, so the Son of Man must be lifted up, that everyone who believes in him may have eternal life."

In Luke Chapter 10:39–41, we read of a disagreement between two sisters. Mary is sitting at the feet of Jesus listening to and absorbing all that Jesus is saying. Martha is busy and distracted by all the preparations that need to be made. She approaches Jesus and asks him to tell Mary to help her, for which she is gently rebuked with Jesus saying, "Mary has chosen what is better."

Sometime later, as recorded in John Chapter 11 Jesus returns to the home of Mary and Martha following the death of their brother Lazarus, having delayed a return visit once, he had heard that Lazarus was not well. Martha believed that Jesus could do miracles and that he could have healed her brother sooner. On the death of her brother Martha's life is at a crossroads. She was overwhelmed by the circumstances of his death and confused as to why Jesus had not come sooner given his ability to bring healing, even suggesting to Jesus that Lazarus would not have died had Jesus been there. So often it is a major problem that brings an awareness of our personal need. Then, in John Chapter 11, we see a turning point for Martha. Up until this point Martha's actions suggest she saw Jesus as a good family friend, someone she liked and was proud to serve. Having promised Martha that Lazarus will rise again, Jesus then challenges Martha on what she believes. He says, "I am the resurrection and the life. He who believes in me will live, even though he dies and whoever lives and believes in me will never die. Do you believe this?" (*John 11:25,26*) She responds by saying, "Yes Lord, I believe that you are the Christ, the Son of God, who was come into the world." (*verse 27*). It was if something had happened in her heart, a light bulb moment. She calls Jesus 'the Christ' and 'the Son of God.' This is a magnificent declaration by Martha.

To believe is to commit in every area of your life. How often have we worked in our own strength and decided in our own minds what it is Jesus should do – and yet he does not do it. If we have committed our life to Him, we have to believe and trust that his response and timing are perfect, something we often only see in hindsight.

What is your response? Is there doubt about who Jesus is to you? Are you overwhelmed by your circumstances? Are you able to make the same magnificent, confident declaration that Martha did?

Jesus is longing to hear your response.

CROSS-OUT

Key Verse: Philippians 2:3. *"Do nothing out of selfish ambition or vain conceit, but in humility consider others better than yourselves."*

Do you remember those times at school when you started to write a piece of work, on a nice clean page in your book and you thought it was all going well when disaster struck, you realised you had spelt a word incorrectly? The only solution was to cross it out neatly. This usually involved a ruler to draw a straight line through the misspelt word. Then you had to write the word correctly above it.

Jesus came to earth to cross out all our wrongs. God had made a perfect world for us but through disobedience in the Garden of Eden, sin entered our world. God needed to draw a line through our sins and cross them out. By dying on the cross, in obedience to his father, that is what Jesus did for each and every one of us. He came to bring forgiveness of our sins, heal our diseases and provide a way back to God. Yes, our sins and disobedience were all crossed out when Jesus stood in our place hanging on the cross.

Jesus also put a line through and crossed out our selfishness. Do you know which letter in the alphabet is the most selfish? It is the letter 'I'. I am sure you have heard children (and some adults) say 'I want, I need, I must have… It is interesting to note that the middle letter of SIN is in fact the letter 'I' too. Can you see that by putting a horizontal line through the letter I, we actually get a cross +. That is exactly what Jesus did, he put a line through our selfishness when he hung on the cross for each of us. "It is finished," are the final words of Jesus on the cross. The debt has been paid. He bore our sins on his body so that we do not have to carry our sins or be burdened by them. We have to die to sin and live in righteousness. Though the letter I is in sin, it is not in love. Jesus stretched out his arms of love on the cross so that the sins of the world would be crossed out.

Sometimes the 'I' comes to the forefront because of pride or we think that we deserve something. So how do we stay humble and unselfish? Our key verse from Philippians Chapter 2 gives a strong contrast between demonstrating selfish ambition or vain conceit with a willingness to show humility, or to consider others better than yourself. Paul is writing to the church in Philippi having received reports that the church there is demonstrating a lack of unity and this is one element of their behaviour which is causing him concern. Similar warnings are expressed by the apostle James. In James 3:14–16, selfish ambition is mentioned twice and linked to envy. James's warning is that these lead to disorder and every evil practice.

The following verses in Philippians 2, where we are exalted to imitate Christ's humility and that our attitude should be the same as Christ Jesus (*Philippians 2:2–4*), show how we can break our selfish nature.

Jesus begins these exultations by saying, "Make my joy complete by,"

v.2; being like-minded:–

by thinking like Christ and knowing him and his word accurately.

v.2; having the same love for each other:–

loving others equally and not having favourites. Not being drawn into cliques and only relating to special friends. There is no place in the Christian body for disunity, jealousy, envy or resentment.

v.2; being one in spirit and purpose:–

we may be different but we are one body. Choose to see the giftedness of fellow believers. We are united by the Spirit and in the Spirit. Our purpose is then to share the good news and preach the gospel to the lost

v.3; doing nothing out of selfish ambition or vain conceit:–

rather than having a desire to put one's self forward, be self-seeking, being of one mind with other believers enables us to put their interests before our own and in a sense enables us to develop an attitude of servanthood that so epitomised the ministry of Jesus.

v.3; consider, in humility others better than yourself:–

being humble means we are not concerned with, or motivated by self-interest and we adopt an attitude of 'preferring others.'

v.4; looking not only to your own interests but the interests of others:–

there is nothing wrong with being ambitious, but when it becomes what is best for us, what we need or want then it is sin.

Jesus' only motive was to please His Father. In the same way we should always check our motive for anything by asking ourselves the following two questions. Does it line up with our Father's will? Will this action glorify God? Sometimes we take on tasks thinking they make good sense but do they make God sense?

We each have to take up our own cross when we walk with Jesus. In Mark 8:34 we read, "If anyone would come after me, he must deny himself and take up his cross and follow me." The cross was an instrument of death and here symbolises the necessity of total commitment by the follower, putting to death his own life in order to follow Jesus.

Paul sums this all up in a couple of verses in his letter to the Galatians.

Chapter 2: 20, "I have been crucified with Christ and I no longer live, but Christ lives in me. The life I live in the body, I live by faith in the Son of God who loved me and gave himself for me."

Chapter 6:14, "May I never boast except in the cross of our Lord Jesus Christ. Through which the world has been crucified to me and I to the world."

So come to the foot of the cross and consider Him and what He has done for you.

DIG

Key verse: Luke 12:34. "For where your treasure is, there will be your heart also."

I am looking out into my garden and there is a hive of activity. The squirrels are gathering hazelnuts from our neighbour's garden and burying them in our lawn. Walking over our lawn is like walking on a cobbled street, very lumpy! I was interested to see how focussed the squirrels are in digging up our lawn in order to bury their treasure. They keep digging and digging and digging until they are satisfied that the hole is deep enough for their hazelnut. Then they covered it, so it was totally hidden. Watching this scenario, my mind was drawn to three verses in Matthew Chapter 13 about a buried treasure and the sudden discovery of a valuable pearl.

Matthew 13:44-46, "The Kingdom of Heaven is like treasure hidden in a field. When a man found it, he hid it again and then in his joy went and sold all he had and bought that field."

"Again the Kingdom is like a merchant looking for fine pearls. When he found one of great value, he went away and sold everything he had and bought it."

Apparently, in these times it was quite common to bury treasure as there were no banks.

The first man actually found the treasure accidentally, but after discovering it he kept it himself and went and sold all his possessions so he could buy the whole field. This is an illustration of how some people have an encounter with God even though they may not actually be looking for him.

The second man though, was a merchant in pearls, so it was his business to buy them. The pearl he found was the treasure of a lifetime. He went and sold all his possessions so he could buy it.

The point of these two illustrations, represented by the treasure and the pearl, is not that money will buy either the treasure or the pearl, but that to enter the Kingdom of God it is worth giving up everything else. The treasure and the valuable pearl were above and beyond the worth of everything they had.

Both stories show the joy of a disciple in finding the Kingdom of God through a relationship with Jesus Christ. They were both willing to give up everything for this.

It all starts with sorting out what we value. In Matthew Chapter 6:19–21 it says, "Do not store up for yourself treasures on earth, where moth and rust destroy and where thieves break in and steal. But store up for yourself treasures in Heaven, where moth and rust do not destroy and where thieves do not break in and steal, for where your treasure is, there your heart will be also."

These verses are saying that a man's treasure only lasts for a certain time, but God's treasure lasts forever. The treasure hidden in the field was there all the time and many people passed by that field daily, but they did not find it. As Christians, we are privileged to know and experience the real treasure, the treasure that is the presence of God in our lives. We dig in the field of the mind and find God's love. We discover the real treasure. We seek to know Him better by digging deeper. The treasure has been hidden by God so that people who seek Him, will find Him.

Matthew 6:33 says, "But seek first His Kingdom and his righteousness and all these things will be given to you as well."

The first thing we have to do is to seek, dig or search. Something within us will initiate this search. There will be a trigger. There will be a feeling within you that spurs you on to find Jesus. Jesus is actually waiting for us. Revelation 3:20 says, "Here I am! I stand at the door and knock. If anyone hears my voice and opens the door I will come in and eat with him and he with me."

We have to turn the handle and invite Him into our hearts.

Back to my squirrel. He knows where to dig for his treasure and he claims it.

Have you found your treasure yet and claimed it?

ENCOURAGE

Key verse: Hebrews 3:13. "Encourage one another daily."

So, what does to encourage mean? It means to provide support, to give confidence or hope to someone about a situation or circumstance and to build self-esteem in others.

One character in the Bible who was renowned for being an encourager was Barnabas. His real name, the name given to him by his parents, was Joseph. He was given the nickname Barnabas which meant 'son of encouragement'. 'Bar' which equates to 'son of' and 'Nabas' which was Hebrew referring to a prophetic exhortation which encouraged or built people up.

There are three particular character traits of Barnabas that prompted others to give him his nickname, 'son of encouragement.'

First, he was a man with a generous spirit. In Acts Chapter 4:37 we read that he, "Sold a field he owned and brought the money to the apostles' feet." People with a generous spirit have a way of lifting the spirits of others.

Second, he was a man who could be trusted, when a new church was established in Antioch the church in Jerusalem sent Barnabas to encourage the new believers. When that same church made a collection for the church in Jerusalem it was Barnabas who was trusted to transport the money.

Thirdly, he was a man who always saw the best in others and used his influence to encourage a similar attitude from others. The prime example of this followed Paul's conversion and subsequent desire to speak to the believers in Jerusalem. Not surprisingly the church in Jerusalem was suspicious of Paul and it was Barnabas who retells the story of Paul's conversion to convince the church that they have nothing to fear.

Barnabas' whole life was guided by the Holy Spirit and he had an unshakeable confidence in God. He spent time with believers encouraging them to remain faithful to God. He was a humble man and there was never any motivation to promote himself, only Jesus. He always put others first. His heart was planted in the eternal kingdom and he was not driven by gathering earthly possessions. He was also willing to take a risk especially with his work with non-believers.

His example should encourage us all today. As followers of Jesus we need to remain committed to serving others for the Glory of God. Barnabas would help and support people. It wasn't an easy ride for him as he came up against hostility and persecution for his preaching and teaching. This did not deter him. Barnabas was not a perfect man but he did live up to his name.

So what characteristics can we glean from the life of Barnabas which will help us to be an encourager?

A genuine love for people.

A listening and sympathetic ear.

An eye for potential.

A constant source of hope.

Being a positive and inspiring example.

In Hebrews Chapter 10:23–25 we read: "Let us hold on unswervingly to the hope we profess, for he who promised is faithful. And let us consider how we may spur one another on towards love and good deeds. Let us not give up meeting together, as some are in the habit of doing, but let us encourage one another – all the more as you see the Day approaching."

There is something about praise and encouragement that, although we may find it hard to believe or accept, never leaves our hearts or minds. Everyone needs an encourager who sees the God-given potential in them and also sees the potential of a living relationship with our Saviour. So be encouraged by Barnabas and encourage someone today!

FOCUS

Key verse: Hebrews Chapter 12: 2a. "Let us fix our eyes
on Jesus, the author and perfector of our faith."

The word focus means to pay attention to, to see clearly and to concentrate on one particular point. Jesus was a man of total focus as we read in John 5:19, "I tell you the truth the Son can do nothing by himself, he can only do what he sees His Father doing, because whatever the Father does the Son also does." Jesus stresses his dependence on knowing the will of his Father. John 10:30 says, "I and the Father are one."

It is so important to keep our focus and fix our eyes on Jesus. He is our spiritual power. In Hebrews 12:2 it says, "Let us fix our eyes on Jesus, the author and perfector of our faith, who for the joy set before him endured the cross, scorning its shame and sat down at the right hand of the throne."

Just as a runner fixes his eyes on the finish line, we should concentrate on Jesus as the goal and objective of our faith. Paul, in writing to the church in Philippi (*Philippians 3:13–14*), encourages the church to forget what is behind them and press on towards what is ahead. To win the prize for which God has called them heavenwards in Christ Jesus. So often, we get drawn into what we see happening around us rather than fixing our eyes on the unseen. Our circumstances of this present life are often painful and perplexing. If we constantly fix our eyes on these, then it will cause us to lose heart. The unseen realities we have as Christians are eternal and imperishable, the circumstances of this world are temporary and fleeting.

In the Bible we see people totally committed and focused on Jesus.

Paul, for example, was the Pharisee of Pharisees before his sudden conversion on the road to Damascus. After his conversion, where he had laid down his own life for Jesus, Paul knew his goal was to present the gospel to the Gentiles. He had been chosen by God to do this for in Acts 9:15 we read, "This is my chosen instrument." Knowing God was at the heart of his ambition. Paul didn't let the baggage of his past dictate his future. He wasn't going to waver. He had total focus.

As Christians, our focus should constantly and entirely be on Jesus. We often start off our Christian journey full of good intent, but then the things of life seem to get in the way, we become distracted by the things going on around us and our focus on Jesus becomes blurred. I am reminded of the Parable of the Sower in Matthew Chapter 13.

In the parable, the farmer sowing the seed represents God who is attempting to sow the seed into our hearts. What type of soil is in our hearts will determine whether His word will flourish. So, we have seed falling on the path, seed falling on rocky ground, seed falling amongst thorns and seed falling on fertile soil. The seeds falling on the path and the rocky ground fail to grow. The seeds sown amongst the thorns became plants, but they were eventually choked by the weeds, which represented the distractions and pressures we all face. It can be like that for us when we try to keep focused on Jesus. It is only in the fertile soil that the seeds germinate and produce an abundant crop. The main message from the Parable of the Sower is that unless we nurture our relationship with God in the good soil, we will not grow into the faithful Christians he calls us to be. We feed our faith through God's word and by seeking him earnestly.

If we are feeling our focus is becoming rather blurred and we realise our lives have other foci, which have become more important to us than Jesus then we need to STOP and take a moment to realign ourselves to our true focus. Rather like a telescope that goes out of focus adjustment is needed. John, when writing to the church in Ephesus (*Revelation 2:4*) admonished them for, "having forsaken their first love." The church had lost its focus on Jesus and supporting each other.

If we have an internal foundation built on the cross of Christ, then external changes in our lives will not affect us, as we are rooted and grounded in God. The many storms we have in our lives do help us to grow spiritually, as we put our trust in Jesus he will carry us through.

So how do we keep focused? Jesus is our example. When he felt he wasn't totally focused on his Father he withdrew from his disciples and the crowds to be alone with His Father and spent time in prayer. Maybe we need to do the same. Be alone with Our Father.

Remind yourself :-

a) God loves you unconditionally.

b) God is good to you,

c) God will provide for you.

d) God understands your situation

e) God is greater than your circumstances.

For each of these we should thank God. It isn't until we stop and remind ourselves of these that we can see how much God has already done for us. This will help us re-adjust our focus back on Him.

We also need to, "pray continually" (*1 Thessalonians 5:16*) and read our Bibles daily and try to limit our distractions.

We all need a focal point in our lives, a purpose. The focal point of spiritual power is The Cross. If we stay connected to this centre of power, its energy will be released in our lives. As the words of the song written by Helen Lemmel say:

'Turn your eyes upon Jesus

Look full in His wonderful face,

And the things of earth

Will grow strangely dim

In the light of His Glory and Grace.'

We can all have a purposeful abundant life if we keep our focus on Jesus.

GO

Key verse: Matthew 28:19, "Therefore, go and make disciples of all nations."

In Matthew 28:18,19, there are two quite well known verses, often referred to as the Great Commission. It is where we are commanded to go out and share Jesus with others.

"All authority in heaven and on earth has been given to me. Therefore go and make disciples of all nations."

So how do we do that? Do you feel ready for the challenge? Do you feel equipped for the challenge?

It's rather like sitting at a set of traffic lights. The red light is on, so we are waiting; then it's red and amber so we get ready; and finally what we have been waiting for, the lights turn green. Off we go! Oh dear, the car is in gear but when we press the accelerator nothing happens. What's wrong? We realise that we have no fuel in the tank and without that, no power (or coming up to date we forgot to plug it into the electric charging point).

So what is the power we need? We need to be filled with the Holy Spirit otherwise we are powerless. In Acts 1:4–5, Jesus says to his disciples, "Do not leave Jerusalem, but wait for the gift my Father promised, which you have heard me speak about. For John baptised with water, but in a few days you will be baptised with the Holy Spirit."

In Acts Chapter 20 we read that Paul meets with the elders of the Ephesian church to explain why he is travelling on to Jerusalem. He says to them (*verse 22*), "And now, compelled by the Spirit, I am going to Jerusalem, not knowing what will happen to me there." Then, despite the dangers he may face he says to the elders, (*verse 24*), "However, I consider my life worth nothing to me, if only I may finish the race and complete the task the Lord Jesus has given me – the task of testifying to the gospel of God's grace."

Two things strike me about these statements by Paul. Firstly, that his actions are in direct response to a prompting by the Holy Spirit and secondly, that despite knowing that prison and hardships await him, he is confident that he will triumph as a witness because of the power of the same Holy Spirit.

Earlier in Chapter 14 of the book of John, (*verse 26*), we read about God's promise of a Helper, "But the Counsellor, the Holy Spirit, whom the Father will send in my name, will teach you all things and will remind you of everything I have said to you."

These verses show us that unless we are filled with the Holy Spirit then we do not have the resources to complete the command in the Great Commission. In Ephesians 5:18 it clearly says, "Be filled with the Spirit." This is not a one-off occurrence as we need a continual filling of the Holy Spirit.

Jesus, in Luke 4:18, shows us that He knows that the Holy Spirit is upon Him. He says, "The Spirit of the Lord is upon me because He has anointed me to preach good news to the poor. He has sent me to proclaim freedom for the prisoners and recovery of sight to the blind and to release the oppressed."

In order to walk in the power of the Holy Spirit we need to be connected to the source – which is a relationship with Jesus. Otherwise, we work in vain. I was reminded of this one day when I was drying my hair with a hairdryer. I thought it was fully plugged into the socket, but when I checked there was a small gap between the plug and the socket, so I had to give it a little nudge to make the connection complete. As soon as I did this the hairdryer began to work at full power. Maybe we need to check that we are properly and fully connected to the source of power, or do we need the little nudge to push ourselves that bit closer.

Jesus ministered to people in the power of the Holy Spirit. If we are followers of Jesus this same Holy Spirit is available to us. We need to ask God to fill us with His Holy Spirit. Have you asked Him?

James 4:2 says, "You do not have because you have not asked."

Someone else in the Bible, Philip, was told to 'Go' by the Lord. This can be found in Acts 8:26. An angel visited Philip and told him to go south down the desert road. Right away he set off. The word 'Go' had spurred Philip into action. The word 'Go' does require an action. He was to meet an Ethiopian eunuch, who was an important official, travelling in a chariot. Philip caught up with the chariot and heard the Ethiopian reading scripture. Philip joined him in the chariot and was able to explain what the scriptures meant. The outcome of Philip being obedient to the call of the Spirit, was that Philip baptised the Ethiopian official and he became a follower of Jesus.

If Philip hadn't taken any action when he heard the word 'Go' then the Ethiopian eunuch would have been a lost soul.

Luke 10:1-3, is an account of Jesus sending out his 72 followers to reap the harvest of people. Jesus says, "Go, I am sending you out." Nothing happens until we respond to the call to go.

So where is our harvest field? Do I have to go to Africa to be a missionary? The answer is of course, no. Our missionary field is where we live. Maybe start by praying every time you go out locally "Lord, who do you want me to speak to today?" You will be amazed the different people you will encounter and different situations that you will come across. God will lead you by his Holy Spirit. We are to be His witnesses every day. It is how we are to live. Jesus said in Acts1:8, after telling his disciples that they would receive power through the Holy Spirit, that they, "Will be my witnesses in Jerusalem, in all Judea and Samaria and to the end of the earth. In other words, wherever you go.

I was thinking that as disciples of Jesus, if we tell one person about Him what would the knock- on effect be? It is a bit like this 'R' number we kept hearing about during the Covid epidemic. How many people we could infect if we had the disease. Maybe we should think how many people we could infect with Jesus. Just a thought!

There may also be consequences if we choose to ignore the call to 'Go'. You will recall that Jonah was told by God to go to the city of Nineveh. So what did Jonah do? He headed off in the opposite direction, to Tarshish. Not a wise move, as he ended up in the belly of a large fish. After saving Jonah, God again spoke to him and thankfully this time he obeyed the call to 'Go'.

There is a significance in when God may tell you to 'Go'. It will be just at the right time as God's timing is perfect. We read in Romans 5:6 that Jesus died just at 'the right time' for us. Our timing and thought processes are often far away from God's. God knows the plans He has for you. His plans are always good.

In Jeremiah 29:11, we read, "For I know the plans I have for you, declares the Lord, plans to prosper you and not to harm you, plans to give you hope and a future."

Revelation 22:13 says of God, "I am the Alpha and Omega, the First and the Last, the Beginning and the End."

Alpha is the first letter of the Greek alphabet and Omega is the last. He knows the beginning and the end.

So if you hear God's voice and He says Go, are you ready?

Checklist:–

I have a relationship with Jesus.

I have been filled with His Holy Spirit.

I am ready to go willingly to glorify His Name.

Just remember, with God there is no such thing as retirement.

HUMBLE

Key verse: James 4:6. "God opposes the proud but gives Grace to the humble."

To be humble, or to exhibit humility, is not a quality often seen in our world today. Our world probably displays the exact opposite – out for oneself. I am the most important one! It's all about me! Often being humble is equated with being weak – being a doormat and allowing everyone to walk all over you. Far from it. Being humble means being modest or unpretentious. You are aware of your shortcomings. Holman's Bible Dictionary defines humility as 'the personal quality of being free from arrogance and pride and having an accurate estimate of one's worth.' The real purpose of humility is to help us to understand where we are in our relationship with God.

If we have given our lives to Jesus, then we should live in humble holiness. We have a heart that realises what Jesus's death on the cross really means. He died for me, even before I knew anything about Him. He completed my salvation. He has forgiven all my sins and I will be with Him in eternity.

Jesus is the best example of someone leading a humble life. Philippians 2: 3–5 says, "Do nothing out of selfish ambition or vain conceit, but in humility consider others better than yourselves. Each of you should look not only to your own interests but the interests of others. Your attitude should be the same as that of Christ Jesus." Jesus, as recorded at the beginning of Matthew Chapter 18 asks his disciples, "Who is the greatest in the kingdom of heaven?" (*verse 1*). Having asked the question the following verses outline Jesus's practical response to his own question. "He called a little child and had him stand among them. And he said, 'I tell you the truth, unless you change and become like little children, you will never enter the kingdom of heaven. Therefore, whoever humbles himself like this child is the greatest in the kingdom of heaven.'" *(Matthew 18:2–4)*

Being humble is the source of Christian unity and the way for all of us to live in harmony with each other. We need to have the right attitude and to see others worthy of preferential treatment – this is Christian love, we should honour and prefer one another. There should be no selfish ambition or wanting to promote yourself. We need the self-sacrificing humility that Jesus displayed and love for one another.

Beware those who exhibit a false humility, who promote a false image of themselves or their circumstances, often to curry favour or who are using such statements to further their own ends. Ask God for a spirit of discernment to help you identify false humility.

Our key verse, James 4:6 stated, "God opposes the proud but gives Grace to the humble."

This was written at a time when the Christians were committing several sins and not living in unity. There was quarrelling, murder, adultery, lust, greed and envy. This verse was a reprimand. In the following verses James lays out three ways on how they can restore their relationship with God.

1. Resist the devil and he will flee.
2. Draw near to God – be single-minded about your commitment to Him and do not be tossed about.
3. Humble yourself and He will exult you.

It is so important to humble yourself before Him when you know you have strayed.

In 2 Chronicles 7:14 we read, "If my people, who are called by my name, will humble themselves and pray and seek my face and turn from their wicked ways, then I will hear from Heaven and forgive their sin and heal their land."

Humility is actually a characteristic that all Christians should display. Humility always blossoms in the heart of a person who loves God, as they are walking in Spirit and Truth – admitting a lowly heart and the greatness of God, acknowledging His Majesty. Without the Lord we can do nothing.

So try to keep a humble heart by walking close to God in your life and you will be amazed by how many people will see this quality in you and be drawn to God.

INVITE

Key verse: Luke 14:1. "A certain man was preparing a great banquet and invited many guests."

This quotation is taken from The Parable of the Great Banquet as told by Jesus whilst he is sitting at the table in the home of a prominent Pharisee, having been invited to a Sabbath meal.

In response to a statement by one of the guests (*Luke 14:15*), Jesus begins telling those present that once the banquet is ready the man sends his servant to tell the invitees that everything is ready and that they should come. It was customary at the time to send an early invitation well in advance of the banquet and then a second invitation when all was ready, so all had an opportunity to order their business around the banquet.

How do you think that you might feel on receiving an invite to a great banquet? This is not just a supper or dinner, it will be a sumptuous feast. The important thing is to reply showing acceptance of the invitation, so that the host can know how many of his invites have been accepted and can prepare adequate food to feed them all. You would then, probably, make a note in your diary so as not to miss such an occasion.

But those approached begin to make excuses, as recorded in verses 18–20 of Luke Chapter 14. The first said, "I have just bought a field and I must go and see it. Please excuse me." Another said, "I have just bought five yoke of oxen and I'm on my way to try them out. Please excuse me." Still another said, "I have just got married, so I can't come." These appear to be quite lame excuses and quite likely similar to excuses made by other invited guests. Whatever their real reasons the humiliation and hurt felt by the host would be considerable.

The servant comes back and reports this to his master who is understandably angry given the unanimous rejection by his peers and this rude affront to his hospitality. He then orders his servant, "Go out quickly into the street and alleys of the town and bring in the poor, the crippled, the blind and the lame." (*Luke 18:21*). This list of guests is identical to that Jesus had suggested to his host earlier as recorded in Luke 8:13, those who could not repay him by inviting him in return, in direct contrast to the socially acceptable and rich Pharisees seated around the table with Jesus.

Anticipating what his master would say the servant reports; 'Sir, what you have ordered has been done, but there is still room."

Then the master told his servant, "Go out to the roads and country lanes and make them come in, so that my house will be full" (*Luke 14:23*). Although clearly angry, such a command by the host to invite those of a lower social class, would have been unthinkable at the time.

In this parable, the host represents God the Father and the Banquet Hall is the Kingdom of God. The invited guests are the people of Israel, specifically the Pharisees and Jewish leaders who will plot against Jesus and eventually have him executed as a common criminal. The poor, crippled, blind and lame are the common people regarded as unclean by the Pharisees.

The man holding the feast was determined to fill the house. I wonder how God feels when people reject his invite? I think he is probably grief-stricken at being rejected. He knows that some people will reject his invite. In John 15:18, Jesus is recorded as saying, "If the world hates you, remember it hated me first." God gave us free will to choose, but we will be held responsible for our decisions.

This parable reminds us that we are all invited to the banquet and that the banquet is ready. Sadly, many people are so preoccupied with their own expectations and understanding of the Kingdom that they are unwilling to accept God's invitation, but the invitation still stands. It is a universal invitation with no one left out. All people in society.

If we do not reply or make an excuse, then the Bible is very clear that we will not even get a taste of the Kingdom of Heaven. Luke Chapter 14:24 says, "I tell you, not one of those men who were invited will get a taste of my banquet."

Have you made a decision for Christ and what He did on the cross for you?

Acts Chapter 4:12 says, " Salvation is found in no one else, for there is no other name under Heaven given to men by which we must be saved."

Most invitations have RSVP at the bottom, as does this invitation from God. Don't forget to reply.

JUDGE

*Key verse: Matthew 7:1. "Do not judge or you
too will be judged."*

In the Bible, there are several scriptures about judging. This first one, our key verse, is taken from the Sermon on the Mount where Jesus is sitting down on the mountainside and addressing the crowds who had been following him.

Jesus then continues, in verses 2–5 by saying, "For in the same way as you judge others, you will be judged and with the measure you use, it will be measured to you. Why do you look at the speck of sawdust in your brother's eye and pay no attention to the plank in your own eye? How can you say to your brother, 'Let me take the speck out of your eye, when all the time there is a plank in your own eye?' You hypocrite, first take the plank out of your own eye and then you will see clearly to remove the speck from your brother's eye."

This is a widely quoted passage, but what is it saying? The word judge here actually means to condemn. Jesus is saying is that we are unable to see into a person's heart, only God can do that. It is as if we are taking God's place and making the judgement. We cannot know their motives or the circumstances that have led to what they are saying or doing. We should be humble, knowing our own weaknesses and sins. We judge people on the basis of our own opinions and ideals and often with a critical spirit, we feel superior to them. This is not a Godly judgement. So often we are unaware of our own shortcomings. Jesus describes them as a plank. This is exaggerated so as to compare with the speck in someone

else's eye. We judge the trivial things in others rather than being more concerned about the serious defects we have ourselves. We are very good at nitpicking other's faults. When you judge others you are actually heaping judgement on yourself.

Romans 2:1 is another direct passage about judging others. "You therefore have no excuse, you who pass judgement on someone else."

We, as humans, are very good at seeing faults in others but never seeing our own faults. So often we can become very self-righteous. Everybody else is guilty but we are not. We measure people by our standards, not God's. His judgement is based on the truth.

Luke 6:37 also emphasises that we should not judge (condemn) others. "Do not judge and you will not be judged. Do not condemn and you will not be condemned. Forgive and you will be forgiven."

If we do judge others, we will be judged in exactly the same way. Who of us dare to stand before God and say, "My God, judge me as I have judged others."

One Chronicles 28:9 says, "For the Lord searches every heart and understands every motive behind the thoughts."

Jesus did not relieve his followers of the need for discerning right from wrong, but he condemned unjust and hypocritical judging of others.

The last scripture I want to look at is John 8:3–11. Jesus is at the temple courts when he is approached by the teachers of the law and a group of Pharisees, bringing with them a woman caught in adultery. They make the woman stand in front of Jesus and those around Jesus and then ask Jesus this question, "Teacher, this woman was caught in the act of adultery. In the law Moses commanded us to stone such women. Now what do you say?" They were using this question as a trap in order to have a basis for accusing Him. But Jesus bent down and started to write on the ground with his finger. When they kept on questioning him, he straightened up and said to them, "If any one of you is without sin, let him be the first to throw a stone at her." Again he stooped down and wrote on the ground. At this, those that heard began to go away one at a time, the older ones first, until only Jesus was left with the woman still standing there. Jesus straightened up and asked her, "Woman, where are they? Has no-one condemned you?" "No-one, sir," she replies. "Then neither do I condemn you." Jesus declared. "Go now and leave your life of sin."

The Teachers of the law and the Pharisees here had only one motive, that was to trick Jesus with a dilemma. If Jesus had said to show mercy to her then he would have been in opposition to the law. If he had recommended stoning, then his judgement would conflict with the civil law of Rome. We don't know what he wrote on the ground but it must have made the accusers feel uncomfortable. Jesus also made it clear that he was not going to pronounce judgement on her. When he asked the one without sin to throw the first stone the accusers soon realised that their own condemnation was being recorded. They perceived that they had been judged by the inner motives of their hearts. Jesus had made them realise the moral significance of what they had done. Maybe the older men left first as they realised the wrong motives in their lives over all the years.

He showed mercy and compassion to the woman but did not condone her sin, as he told her to leave her life of sin.

So let's always pause before we open our mouths to say anything that is judgemental or condemning of others. Check our thoughts and motives, because ultimately we all are going to be judged for our thoughts, our words and deeds. No-one has the right to throw stones.

KEEP

Key Verse: Luke 2:19. "Mary treasured up all these things and pondered them in her heart."

The word keep means to retain or hold on to something. These can be actual physical items or memories of an event in the past, which we store in our hearts and minds. They are things that we treasure or hold dear. We want to preserve these events from perishing or being lost.

In both our key verse and in verse 51 of Luke Chapter 2 we are told that Mary, the mother of Jesus, held on to certain moments in her heart and that she, "Treasured all these things in her heart."

Mary had the most remarkable events happen in her life. Quite an unbelievable story as her whole life was turned upside down. She pondered on all that had happened to her and was trying to make sense of it all. There was the visit of the angel Gabriel to tell her she was going to have a baby, God's Son. Then, after Jesus was born, the shepherds came and were talking about the angel's message and how a great number appeared praising God. They talked about the baby being a gift from God to all people and that he would bring peace on earth. As she sat and reflected on all the events that had occurred, she realised that God was in the whole situation and that the baby was a gift from God. Mary held all these divine revelations in her heart and treasured them. Mary cultivated a quiet trusting spirit. This was the foundation of her character. She had a silent inner power of His presence. There was a hushed awe about her. She was a thinker who pondered things over and thought them through. Once all these extraordinary things had been treasured in her heart, she would then be able to recall them at a later date.

Mary must have had many special memories as she watched Jesus grow up. The people he healed and the knowledge of the scriptures as he taught. Most poignant of all was watching Jesus crucified, her sadness turning to joy on the day she knew he had risen from the dead. She saw and witnessed the whole of his life. When it says that Mary pondered these words it means she reflected on them, meditated, examined and weighed them up.

I think we can learn a lot from Mary's example. Often, in our hearts, we not only store the good memories, but certain events that were difficult and bad in our lives. There may be certain people stored there who bring very negative and bad thoughts. Sometimes we need to do some weeding in our own hearts and get rid of any anger or spite that may be there. A heart full of gratitude has no room for spite or anger. A divided mind will divide the heart. We need to bring these bad memories we have before God in prayer and seek forgiveness for our attitude towards these people and situations. We also need to spend time in His word and fill our hearts with His truth. The confidence we have in God comes from the treasures we keep in our hearts.

God speaks words over our lives and we need to bring them to the forefront of our thoughts and meditate and ponder them. Do we need to act on these now or put them away and keep them for later. We owe it to God to treasure and ponder all that He has said to us. The story of Simeon (*Luke 2:25–32*), is an amazing example of someone who had received a word from God, through the Holy Spirit, that he would not die until he had seen the Lord's Christ. His prayer of praise on the fulfilment of that promise is now recorded as the Nunc Dimittis in the *Book of Common Prayer*.

"Lord, now lettest thy servant depart in peace according to thy word.

For mine eyes have seen thy salvation which thou hast prepared before the face of all peoples:

To be a light to lighten the Gentiles and to be the glory of the people Israel."

I want to finish this section with a scripture from Philippians 4: 8,9, with the words of Paul, "Finally, brothers, whatever is true, whatever is noble, whatever is right, whatever is pure, whatever is lovely, whatever is admirable – if anything is excellent or praiseworthy – think about such things. Whatever you have learned or received or heard from me, or seen in me- put into practice. And the God of Peace will be with you."

This passage is a diet for us, it enables us to keep our minds, our bodies and spirits as Jesus would want. The diet consists of:-

1. Truthful things – grounded in God's Word.

2. Honourable things – respect.

3. Right things – they reflect righteousness.

4. Pure things – nothing unclean.

5. Lovely things – beautiful sights, sounds and relationships.

6. Admirable things – people who inspire.

7. Excellent things – encourages us.

8. Praiseworthy things – praising God for everything and breaking the negatives in our minds.

We have a choice, so let's try and feed on the diet.

LOVE

Key verse: 1 John 4:16. "God is love. Whoever lives in love lives in God and God lives in him."

Probably the most quoted passage on love in the Bible is in 1 Corinthians 13:3–8. This is usually spoken at weddings. "Love is patient, love is kind. It does not envy, it does not boast, it is not proud. It is not rude, it is not self-seeking, it is not easily angered. It keeps no record of wrongs. Love does not delight in evil, but rejoices with the truth. It always protects, always trusts, always hopes, always perseveres. Love never fails."

This is part of a letter, written by Paul, to the church in Corinth where there was much unrest and quarrelling. He was really chastising the Corinthian church for not sharing the love of God.

In the Greek language there are four main interpretations to the word love used in the Bible.

Philia – friendship.

Eros – romantic sexual love.

Storge – love between parent and child.

Agape – unconditional love (no strings attached).

Agape is the love that Jesus exhibited and it is only possible to demonstrate this form of love when we are filled with the Holy Spirit and living in the power of the indwelling Christ.

In John 10:30 Jesus talks about how His Father's love for Him was perfect. He says, "I and the Father are one," which says everything about their unity – a relationship based on love.

Jesus makes another amazing statement in John 15: 9, "As the Father has loved me so I love you. Now remain in my love." This perfect love that Jesus has he wants for us through a relationship with Him. God guided and led Jesus while He was here on earth and Jesus wants to do the same for us – how amazing is that!

John 3:16 is also a very well-known verse. "For God so loved the world that He gave His one and only Son, that whoever believes in Him shall not perish but have eternal life."

God demonstrated his own love for us, while we were still sinners, allowing Christ to die for us on the cross.

The story of the Prodigal Son (The Lost Son) in Luke 15:11–31, is a parable to show us all how much God loves every one of us. It is the story about a father and his two sons. The two sons both lived at home. The younger son decided to ask his father for his share of his inheritance. Now an inheritance was only given after someone had died, so this was very unusual. I wonder how much that hurt the father. The younger son then left home and squandered all the inheritance on wild living. When his life hit rock bottom he began to realise what he had done so he decided to return home. He believed that even the hired workmen at home had a better life than he was having. It says that he came to his senses. He realised he had to go back and seek his father's forgiveness for what he had done. He journeyed back home. His father was obviously looking out each day for him because he ran to meet his son even when he was a long way off. It was as if the father had always kept a light on in the house expecting his return one day. He threw his arms around his son and kissed him. The son confessed the wrong he had done and said he was not worthy to be his son. The father's reaction was to throw party. He lavished his love on his son by giving him a robe (a sign of distinction and that he was to be honoured), a ring (a sign of authority) and sandals (freedom.)

This was a total expression of agape love, the unconditional love. When agape love comes towards you, you can run but not hide.

What about the older brother? His attitude was one of resentment towards his brother. He had been at home doing all the work and hadn't disobeyed his father, yet there was party for his younger brother. This parable paints a story for all of us. The younger brother, the prodigal son, represents us, who are sinners. The elder brother represents the righteous man. The father represents God. This parable and the other two parables in Luke 15 (The Lost Sheep and the Lost Coin), illustrate the unconditional love of God for us. God's hunger for the return of sinners and the desire for the righteous to love other people with His agape love. Like the father in the parable, He is always waiting for you to return, day and night. We have, like the younger brother, a moment when we come to our senses and realise that we are all sinners and need to seek God's forgiveness. Often it is only when we are at rock bottom and our world has fallen apart that we reach that point. A recognition of our sin is the beginning of salvation.

The elder son had all he needed at home and did exactly what his father asked of him, but he still needed to be forgiven for his resentment and judgement of his younger brother. It is interesting when the elder son went out to speak to his father he referred to his brother as 'this son of yours' not my brother. His whole attitude was like that of a Pharisee. Rather than rejoicing that an outcast had been found and that he was receiving a blessing from his father, his narrow view on life was that his brother had not kept to the rules of inheritance and that he did not merit any reward when he returned. The elder brother was blind to what had happened to his younger brother and failed to understand the father's love. So often we think that just because we are good and live by all the rules, we will automatically be accepted by the Father. It is not until we realise that we are all sinners and fall short of the glory of

God and it is not until we confess that we are sinners and seek His forgiveness that are we accepted by the Father. God is waiting for you to come back to Him, as the father waited for his lost son to return.

What lessons can we learn from the parable?

Are we living like the younger or elder son?

Is there a hunger in you to return to the Father?

Are we offended when 'outcasts' come to the Father and receive all the blessings? Do we feel that is unfair and resentment fills our whole being?

The Pharisees always complained that Jesus spent a lot of time with the outcasts – people not like us! He even touched lepers!

I expect at some point in our lives we have all felt resentment and the 'it's not fair' syndrome. We need to seek forgiveness for our hardened hearts towards people who have received a blessing from the Lord.

We must be aware of our attitude and motives all the time.

Is God calling you back to Himself? He is always waiting for you. Come back to Him today. He will not disappoint you.

MIND – (THE GAP)

Key verse: Isaiah 6:8b. "Here am I. Send me!"

As a child growing up in London, I frequently used the London Underground. As one of the tube trains approached a station there was always a recorded message played over the Tanoy saying, 'Mind the gap'. There was quite a large gap between the platform and the train so everyone had to be very careful when either getting on or alighting from the train. I remember thinking that my foot would have fitted very easily down the gap. Once I had arrived safely on to the train there was a real sense of achievement. I've done it!

So often, in life, there seems a great gap developing in front of us and sometimes these gaps seem like huge chasms. The distance from where we are standing to where we want to go seems unbridgeable. We need to be aware of the gaps happening and to have the determination to close the gap. So often the one gap that usually develops, without us realising it, is the gap between us and God. Somehow it can just sneak up on us. When we first make a commitment to the Lord we feel very close to Him, but as the years roll by that gap can widen. Life happens and our circumstances change, sometimes for the better and sometimes that change brings pressures that consume us. However, it is us that have moved away and created the gap, not God. God is the constant one and He never changes. When we become aware of what has happened then we need to do something about it. We need to have a discipline of spiritual perseverance. Perseverance is more than endurance; it is endurance + assurance + the certainty that it will happen – we will get back and be close to the Lord. We have to consciously make the effort to spend time with God. If you are unsure why the gap has happened then ask God to show you. There may be things in your life that you will have to deal with, circumstances that you need to change, or personal matters that are causing the separation. There is not a gap too big that God cannot close. His desire is to direct us towards Himself and to close the gap.

We can also interpret minding the gap in different ways. In the ancient world, the cities had walls around them to provide protection from enemies. When the walls had been breached the city became vulnerable to destruction. The only way to secure the wall was for men to risk their lives and literally stand in the gap and fight the enemy. So, in the Book of Nehemiah, we read of Nehemiah returning to the city of Nineveh to rebuild it from a state of ruin. As the rebuild begins the people of Nineveh are open to attack through gaps in unfinished walls. Nehemiah records in Chapter 4, verse 13, "Therefore, I stationed some of the people behind the lowest points of the wall at exposed places." Whilst half continued to build, the other half, armed with swords and spears 'stood in the gap.'

Yet another interpretation appears in the book of Ezekiel. The Jews are in exile in Babylon and God becomes increasingly angry at the actions of the Jewish people who are committing robbery, extortion and oppression. In looking for someone to intercede with him and bring the people to repentance, he says to Ezekiel, "I looked for a man among you who would build up the wall and stand before me in the gap on behalf of the land, so I would not have to destroy it, but I found none." God was so upset that he could not find even one person to stand in the gap for him. He was really asking people to stand up for their faith.

The gaps in the city walls could be likened to the gaps that we create between ourselves and God. The gap creates a space where the enemy can enter and this can equally happen in our spiritual lives. The enemy finds our gaps, especially our weak spots and vulnerabilities – unhealed emotional problems, guilt, pride and a lack of faith. The list is endless. Often we make excuses, for example – It's not my gift. Moses's excuse was that he was no good at speaking up and Jeremiah said, "I'm too young."

What is our excuse?

Jesus came to stand in the gap for us, he stretched out His arms to fill the gap between God and us. So what does it mean for us to stand in the gap today? There are many gaps in our families, churches and our nation today which leave people very vulnerable to attack from the enemy. Holes in the walls are symbols of sin or weaknesses that cause a person to fall from their position. We read in Galatians 6:2, "Carry each other's burdens." We have a choice either to criticise or pray. We can be the go-between in these gaps and intercede for these people and situations. We need to pray continually. Ezekiel was looking for just one person to pray but all the prophets had strayed from a holy life, whereas Moses was willing and obedient to God's call, "then I heard the voice of the Lord saying, 'Whom shall I send? And who will go for us.' And I said 'Here I am. Send me.'"(*Isaiah 6:8*).

God is still searching for people who will stand up for their faith. It takes courage, boldness and a willingness to fight the enemy. It takes just one person to pray to make a difference to a situation. Identify the cause and then pray with authority.

As Christians we need to stand firm with the armour of God on us, which He provides for us, remember this is a spiritual battle we are fighting. As we are in a battle we need to be protected.

Ephesians chapter 6:11,12 says, "Put on the full armour of God so that you can take your stand against the devil's schemes." Think of it as your new wardrobe!

The following verses in Ephesians 6 verses 14–17 continue by saying, "Stand firm then with the belt of truth buckled round your waist, with the breastplate of righteousness in place. In addition to all this, take up the shield of faith, with which you can extinguish all the flaming arrows of the evil one. Take the helmet of salvation and the sword of the Spirit, which is the word of God."

1. Belt of truth.

2. Breastplate of righteousness.

3. Shoes of the gospel of peace.

4. Shield of faith.

5. Helmet of salvation.

6. Sword of the Spirit.

Notice that only one of these garments is to be used in attack – the sword of the spirit. The rest of the garments are to be used in defence against the enemy.

So let's look out for the gaps in our own lives and, for the gaps that God calls us to stand in for Him.

NOURISH

*Key verse: John 6:51. "I am the living bread that
came down from Heaven."*

To nourish is to provide the food necessary for life and growth.

Jesus referred to himself as "The Bread of Life" in John 6:35. He said, "I am the Bread of Life. He who comes to me will never go hungry and he who believes in me will never be thirsty."

Bread is a staple diet in many countries and Jesus is saying that He can be the sustenance required in everyone's life.

We need nourishment every day of our lives to survive physically. There is a need for a healthy diet. There is saying that you become what you eat! Not only do we need to eat healthily we need to chew our food well to improve digestion and to enhance our eating experience. This analogy of nourishing the body physically is a mirror image of what we need to do spiritually. We need to feed on the word of God for the word of God is like a banquet containing many courses and the courses may be seen as a variety of promises which we need to eat (read) and chew over (digest carefully). This will then provide us with spiritual energy and hope.

What are these promises set out in the Word of God?

1. There is forgiveness of sin in 1 John 1:9, "If we confess our sins, he is faithful and just and will forgive us our sins and purify us from all unrighteousness."

2. The promise of eternal life in John 10:27,28, "My sheep listen to my voice; I know them and they follow

me. I give them eternal life and they shall never perish, no-one can snatch them out of my hand."

3. The promise of a future hope in Jeremiah 29:11, "For I know the plans I have for you, declares the Lord, plans to prosper you and not to harm you, plans to give you a hope and a future."

4. He will never forsake us. Deuteronomy 31:8, "The Lord himself goes before you and will be with you, he will never leave you nor forsake you. Do not be afraid, do not be discouraged."

These are just a few of the amazing promises of God and our Bible is the storehouse of these promises. We need to hold these in our hearts and allow the Holy Spirit to put a spark in our heart so they come to life within us and change us and we can draw on them whenever we need.

We have to grow in our spiritual journey and mature, just as we do physically through life from babies to mature men and women.

One Peter 2:2 says, "Like newborn babies crave pure spiritual milk, so that by it you may grow up in your salvation, now that you have tasted that the Lord is good."

In this passage, the word crave is interesting. It means there is unrestrained hunger and desire for spiritual food as only a baby can show when he or she is hungry. Do we crave spiritual milk from the Lord?

There is another passage in Hebrews 5:13,14 which says that any who lives on milk alone is still an infant but solid food is for the mature. We have to grow and mature in our faith. We will show wise, sound judgement when we are confronted with difficult situations, something a baby cannot do. Some Christians do not get any further than the baby stage. Where are you in your Christians walk? Have you moved on to solid food yet?

Summing up. We need to have a disciplined diet spending time in His Word, praying regularly and time being still before the Lord in His presence. As with a physical diet sometimes we slip up and start to eat junk food, which is not nutritious. Similarly with a spiritual diet, we can slip up in our discipline. We occasionally need a spiritual health check – what are we reading, what music are we listening to and which friends are we hanging out with for example.

Finally a verse from James 1:4, "Perseverance must finish its work, so that you may be mature and complete, not lacking anything."

Try feasting on the promises of God.

OVERFLOW

*Key verse: John 10:10. "I have come that they may have
life and have it to the full."*

When we think of the word overflow, we think of something
running over, or spilling over the top of a vessel. There is an
excessive abundance.

Jesus wants us to live in His excessive and overflowing
abundance.

I was reminded of this overflowing love from Jesus when
I visited Niagara Falls several years ago. Not only is the water
from the Niagara River constantly falling over the precipice to
the rocks below, but the energy and mighty power of that water
reminded me of the love that Jesus has for each of us. He wants
us to live in this abundance and when we do so God's presence
flows out of us to impact people and situations around us,
guided by the energy and power of the Holy Spirit.

Romans Chapter 15:13 says, "May the God of hope fill you
with all joy and peace as you trust in Him, so that you may
overflow with hope by the power of the Holy Spirit."

Our trust, faith and hope in His atoning work on the cross is
the key to opening the floodgates and all three are exhibited in
us through the abiding presence of the Holy Spirit.

In Matthew 12:34 we read, "For out of the overflow of the
heart the mouth speaks."

What we speak is so important. Our words identify us.

John 7:37–39 records Jesus speaking about a human thirst
with the spiritual living water that comes through belief in him.
"Jesus stood and said in a loud voice, 'If anyone is thirsty let

him come to me and drink. Whoever believes in me, as the scripture has said, streams of living water will flow from within him.' By this he meant the Spirit, whom those who believed in him were later to receive."

Let's just look at the story of the Samaritan Woman (the woman at the well) found in John Chapter 4. Here, Jesus encounters a Samaritan women who has come to draw some water from the well. Interestingly, Jews and Samaritans did not mix, in particular men and women. At first, the woman doesn't realise what Jesus is actually saying to her, as she is operating on a human level about things and Jesus is speaking on a spiritual level.

John Chapter 4 and verses 13 and 14 records Jesus explaining to the Samaritan woman the importance of the spiritual water that only he can provide. "Everyone who drinks this water will be thirsty again, but whoever drinks the water I give him will never thirst. Indeed, the water I give him will become in him a spring of water welling up to eternal life."

Jesus is giving a comparison here. The water the woman wants to draw from the well is to meet a physical need, whereas His living water refers to a spiritual need. Jesus is saying that nothing physical can satisfy a spiritual need. The living water imparts life and leads to eternal life. There is a deeper meaning here. If you have the gift of eternal life, then you will never thirst. Through this living water you can always be in touch with God by His Holy Spirit. Jesus refers to the Holy Spirit as always springing up, welling up and gushing. He is saying that the Spirit within us is an active, powerful and life-giving spring. It is like a fountain within and there is movement and motion. It is not static. This spring within enables us to do more things than our ability would suggest. Eternal life begins when we are born of the Spirit. Jesus is saying to the woman that if she has the Holy Spirit within then she will never thirst again.

How do we live in this overflow? It is like any journey you go on. Before you go you need to check that you have enough fuel for the journey. It is the same for us spiritually. Is our spiritual fuel tank full of the Holy Spirit? As the Holy Spirit flows out of us we need to refill our tank. Ephesians 5:18 says, "Be filled with the Spirit." This means repeatedly not just a once for all experience. The more we give out the more we need to be refilled. This allows us to continually worship and serve our Lord. We need to spend time with God and to ask Him to fill us with His Holy Spirit.

We need to pass this overflow on to others. We can see this happened when Moses passed his overflow on to Joshua. Deuteronomy 34:9 reads, "Now Joshua, son on Nun, was filled with the Spirit of wisdom because Moses had laid his hands on him."

We have to make room for the Holy Spirit in our hearts. So often our hearts are full of fleshly desires. If only we realised that the coming of His Spirit to reside in our heart would bring life, light and health, but unfortunately Jesus is often crowded out. He can be the light inside of us.

Room is made within us by the Holy Spirit, by His Grace we receive His Mercy. His cup overflows into our lives. We are the riverbed and Holy Spirit is the river flowing through us, imparting, radiating and refreshing till our lives are hidden with Christ in God.

PRESENCE

Key verse: Exodus 33:14. "My presence will go with you and I will give you rest."

I had been praying about how I could convey 'presence' to you and the Lord gave me a revelation this morning. I was getting dressed and I had just taken off my dressing gown and I happened to glance at the label. The label read Presence. It was bought at a well-known department store which is now closed. I love this dressing gown as it is cosy, warm and it wraps around me. I felt the Lord saying this is just like my presence.

There is much talk these days about God's presence. There are some very special moments in our lives when we know that God has been with us. It is tangible. I remember one very special moment in my life when our son had laying on of hands for the healing of his leukaemia. As we stood at the altar rail in our local church, my husband and I felt that Jesus had actually walked by us and touched our son. His presence was tangible as if he had entered the church to stand beside us. These moments have been rare in our walk with the Lord but we are encouraged so much by them when they do happen. They are so special, but we are actually called to live by His presence.

We read in many verses in the Bible that God is with us all the time and that he will never leave us or forsake us. One such example is recorded in Joshua 1:5 which says, "I will never leave you or forsake you." His presence is there all the time. His name is Emmanuel, "God is with us," The question becomes, how do we live our everyday lives in his presence? We need to lay every part of the day before Him. We need to read his word and pray every day. Immerse ourselves in him at the beginning of each day. David made it a practice to place God at the forefront of his daily life. In Psalm 16:1 he writes, "Keep me safe O God for in you I take refuge."

We must totally trust God's truth and our faith in his death, burial and resurrection. We need to be reminded daily that he is always with us. So often we think he is not walking with us as we don't 'feel' that he is there. We believe that he has deserted us, but the truth is that he lives within us by his Holy Spirit. Usually, this feeling comes when we have moved away from him. He is the constant one and never changes.

In Luke 8:22–25 we read about Jesus calming the storm, "One day Jesus said to His disciples," " Let's go over to the other side of the lake." So they got into the boat and set out. As they sailed Jesus fell asleep. A squall came down on the lake, so that the boat was being swamped and they were in great danger. The disciples went and woke Jesus saying "Master, Master we are going to drown!" He got up and rebuked the wind and raging waters; the storm subsided and all was calm. "Where is your faith?" he asked the disciples. In fear and amazement they asked one another. "Who is this? he commands even the winds and waters and they obey Him."

How quickly situations can change. One moment it was all calm on the lake and the next moment a storm had come in. The disciples were terror-stricken. The fury of the winds turned their calm day into a terrifying ordeal. During this Jesus was actually asleep in the boat. The disciples had the presence of Jesus with them. Did they forget that he was with them? Also, they were stunned that the wind and waves obeyed him. Did they really understand who Jesus was and that he could do all things. They were challenging the Lord that he did not care about them. Of course he cares about every single person.

Once we understand that he does care and that he is in control, then we can join him and rest with him.

Psalm 91:14–16 are verses which are a confirmation of all the promises of God to those who truly love him and trust him, "Because He loves me," says the Lord, "I will rescue him, for he acknowledges my name. He will call upon me and I will answer him; I will be with him in trouble, I will deliver him and honour him. With long life will I satisfy him and show him my salvation."

Often, we are like the disciples and fail to recognise his presence in the midst of our storms and troubles. We need to find that presence for ourselves and when we do that presence will be enough.

By the power of the Holy Spirit he is with everyone who believes at all times. We never need to call for Jesus to turn up, as he is always present with us. There may be a sudden awareness on our part of his presence. If we are feeling that we don't know his presence is with us then we need to ask him, "What is keeping me from knowing your presence? Why am I so slow to catch a glimpse of your plan? Help me to see you and experience your presence." When we are aware that Jesus is with us then we have total assurance, comfort and courage.

There must be a hunger within us for his presence. Ask him for spiritual eyes to see him and spiritual ears to hear his words.

The storms and crises in our lives reveal the truth about God. Often it is only when we are at rock bottom that we can see the presence of God at work. If God promises to be among the body of Christians, then he will. It all comes back to abiding in his presence.

Wise words are recorded in Proverbs 3:5–6, "Trust in the Lord with all your heart. Lean not on your own understanding. In all your ways acknowledge Him and he will make your paths straight."

In Psalm 105:3,4 we read, "Glory in his holy name; let the hearts of those who seek the Lord rejoice; look to the Lord and his strength seek his face always."

In Psalm 139:7–10, a psalm of thanks, David writes,

"Where can I flee from your Spirit?

Where can I flee from your presence?

If I go up to the heavens you are there;

If I make my bed in the depths you are there.

If I rise on the wings of the dawn,

If I settle on the far side of the sea,

even there your hand will guide me,

your right hand will hold me fast."

We cannot hide from his 'presence', but as these verses record, we can rest in his presence and take comfort in his strength.

QUIET

Key verse: Psalm 46:10. "Be still. And know that I am God."

Quiet is defined as the absence of noise or bustle. So often today we find quiet or silence very difficult. There seems to be an inward desire for noise to fill our day. There is music playing in most of the shops now. People jog and listen to music through their earpieces attached to their mobiles. Why do we find silence and the ability to sit quietly so difficult and feel the need to fill them with some noise? If things fall quiet our immediate reaction is to think that something is wrong, which is a shame as silence can be really powerful in its own right.

These times of quiet though, are necessary for us as they allow us to wait on the Lord and to hear His voice. Psalm 37:7 says, "Be still before the Lord and wait patiently for Him." Psalm 23:2 says, "He leads me beside quiet waters." Our key verse reminds us that in the stillness we can know God. God wants us to rest with Him. When we do He provides rest, refreshment and well-being for our souls. During these quiet times, we learn to build our faith and trust in Him. Having these quiet moments in our lives will quieten all the turmoil going on inside of us and will translate to a peaceful existence and demeanour on the outside.

Isaiah 30:15 says, "In quietness and trust is your strength." We can know that God is our sustainer, provider and defender. These are words of assurance. We all need these times of quiet as God provides these times so we can draw close to Him. In Isaiah 55:6 it says, "Seek the Lord while he may be found." In particular, we are told to seek His face. "Look to the Lord and His strength; seek His face always." (*Psalm 105:4*) His face is the brightness of His character, but this is not always our constant experience. It is often hidden behind our human desires. We are meant to enjoy greatness and beauty at all times.

What does it actually mean to 'seek His face?' It means setting our hearts and minds on God and consciously fixing our attention on Him. It is a conscious choice we have to make. Two Chronicles 7:14 states; "If my people who are called by my name, will humble themselves and pray and seek my face and turn from their wicked ways, then I will hear from Heaven and will forgive their sin and heal their land." His favour flows from His face. In order to seek his face we need some quiet spaces in our lives. In seeking God we need to keep persevering and pursuing his presence. Jeremiah confirms that if we keep seeking him we will find him. Jeremiah Chapter 29:13–14 records, "You will seek me and find me when you seek me with all your heart. I will be found by you, declares the Lord."

In these quiet spaces, when we spend time with the Lord, it helps to build that intimate relationship he requires from us as believers. It is like a wedding when the bride stands beside her husband to be and removes her veil. The couple see each other face to face. Nothing is blocking their relationship.

Interestingly, when Moses came down from the mountain with the two tablets containing the Ten Commandments, his face was radiant, but Moses didn't realise it was. His followers noticed this. It was after speaking with the Lord face to face.

So, these quiet times, God gives us are the building times in our spiritual journey. They are so important with our walk with the Lord. I want to end this section with the benediction that is found in Numbers 6:23–26:–

"The Lord bless you and keep you,
the Lord make His face shine upon you
and be gracious to you;
the Lord turn his face towards you
and give you peace."

RISK

Key verse: Matthew 14:29. "Peter got out of the boat,
walked on the water and came towards Jesus."

What does the word risk conjure up for you? It can convey a sense of adventure, or more likely, uncertainty and a sense of danger. The dictionary defines risk as acting despite the possibility of injury or loss. As Christians, we are all called to take a risk for Jesus. Just look at the life of Jesus, he took many risks – with the words he spoke, the healings he performed in front of a crowd and the places he visited.

When I think of taking a risk I am reminded of Peter. Our key verse begins an account of the time when Peter had enough faith to risk getting out of the boat and to walk on water. This is an example of Peter doing something, with God's help, which he could never have done on his own. Do you want to step out in faith?

So often we believe we have a call from God to step out and put that call into action. Then fear begins to set in – it's too scary, you feel inadequate, there is fear of failure and a fear of letting God down. God does reassure us every step of the way. If we look at Moses in the book Exodus, he felt inadequate because he had a stutter and in Exodus Chapter 4:10 he expresses this inadequacy to the Lord, "O Lord I have never been eloquent, neither in the past nor since you have spoken to your servant. I am slow of speech and tongue." In verse 12 the Lord responds by saying, "I will help you speak." Just as the Lord tries to reassure Moses, there are many other examples of God encouraging others to overcome their uncertainty and to step out in faith. Think of Abraham, Gideon, David and Paul.

Let's go back to Peter in Matthew Chapter 14. The disciples were out on the lake when a storm arose and they were being buffeted by the wind. The disciples then saw Jesus walking on the water. They were afraid and Jesus said to them, "Take courage it is I. Do not be afraid" (*verse 27*). Then Peter called out to Jesus and said, "Lord if it is you tell me to come to you on the water." "Come," said the Lord." (*verses 28 and 29*).

Peter was always an impulsive person, saying things which he hadn't thought through, so why did he ask the Lord to confirm who he was and ask Him to call him. He probably had learnt from his past mistakes to make sure it was a call from the Lord. So often people make foolish and reckless decisions on their own without checking that it is part of God's plan for their life. Peter was just checking it was Jesus's will for him to get out of the boat and not one of his reckless whims. So Peter stepped out of the boat. He was fine at first, but then in verse 30 it says, "When he saw the wind he was afraid and began to sink." He cried out, "Lord save me." The wind was probably strong when he started, but he didn't notice it as his eyes were fixed on Jesus. At that point, fear set in and he began to sink. He had taken his eyes off Jesus and was focused on the difficulties surrounding him. Jesus response was, "You of little faith, why did you doubt?" (*verse 31*). He was really saying, "Fear not, I am with you." Immediately Jesus reached out his hand and caught him.

There are 366 verses in the Bible using the words 'fear not'. Fear is a warning cry that danger is nearby and we had better do something about it. Initially, when Peter got out of the boat Jesus gave him the power to walk on the water, but as soon as Peter's eyes and thoughts moved away from Jesus, he began to sink, but he did not drown as Jesus was there to catch him. Jesus never calls us out of our comfort zones in order to fail. So often we are like Peter and weigh up all the problems around us and think it is impossible to achieve the risk we have taken.

When we step out of our comfort zone, initially there is excitement and everything clicks into place and we are thriving spiritually. More often than not, in reality, this does not happen. Usually, there are setbacks and times of waiting to take the next step. The hardest thing is to wait. What God does while we are waiting is as important as what we are waiting for. We have to be patient and trust in the Lord. God often calls us to come out of our comfort zone. If we are obedient to this call we will be amazed at the blessings that follow and the potential in us that is unearthed. Faith, itself, means taking risks.

As Peter and Jesus got back into the boat, the wind died down. This whole episode spoke to all the disciples as their response in Matthew 14:32 records. "Truly you are the Son of God," and they worshipped Him. Their worship grew deeper after this whole experience. That is true for us too, as we trust Jesus, our worship of Him will grow deeper and deeper.

God promises to be with us when we take a risk and step out for Him. We read in Joshua 1:9, "Do not be terrified, do not be discouraged for the Lord your God will be with you wherever you go." We need to totally trust the Lord and keep our focus on Him.

In Isaiah 26:4 we read, "Trust in the Lord forever, for the Lord, the Lord is the Rock eternal."

God gives us freedom to decide whether or not we will take risks for him. If we say yes often it will be a wobbly journey but through it your life will be changed. If you only venture into the unknown when everything is safe you may be waiting a long time.

SEAL

Key verses: Ephesians 1:13,1. "And you also were included in Christ when you heard the word of truth, the gospel of salvation. Having believed you were marked in him with a seal, the promised Holy Spirit, who is a deposit guaranteeing our inheritance until the redemption of those who are in God's possession – to the praise of his glory."

In olden days, when letters were sent, a wax seal was put at the end of the letter with an impression of the writer's signet ring to show the authentication of the letter. It was an official confirmation of approval. Today we may say that something has 'my seal of approval'.

In 2 Corinthians 1:21 we read, "Now it is God who makes you and us stand firm in Christ. He anointed us and set his seal of ownership on us and put his Spirit in our hearts as a deposit, guaranteeing what is to come."

This sealing brings many blessings to us, security, authenticity, ownership and authority. By giving us the Holy Spirit, God seals or stamps us as His own at our conversion. Then the Holy Spirit continues to testify, authenticating this relationship, by making us more and more like Jesus. God, who has authenticated this relationship, will protect his people through trials and difficulties. He will do this until he takes final possession of us, his inheritance on the day of redemption, which is at the end. To be sealed with the Holy Spirit is the gracious gift of God, where he demonstrates his ownership, authority and commitment to his people.

We are sealed by his Holy Spirit the moment we are converted, yet many Christians do not realise this. They also seem to know very little about the Holy Spirit. The Holy Spirit is the third person of the Trinity – Father, Son and Holy Spirit. They are one and co-equal – Triune God. Not all believers are living filled and controlled lives by the Spirit's power. When we first believe we have the Holy Spirit, but we are filled with the Holy Spirit when we submit the whole of our lives to Him.

How does the Holy Spirit help us in our everyday lives?

The Holy Spirit will;–

1. Guide us into the Truth.
    John 16:13 states, "But when he, The Spirit of Truth comes, he will guide you into all truth. He will not speak on his own; he will speak only what he hears and he will tell what is yet to come."

2. Guide and direct our steps.
    In Romans 8:9-11 we read, "You, however, are not controlled by the sinful nature but by the Spirit, if the Spirit of God lives in you. And if anyone does not have the Spirit of Christ he does not belong to Christ. But if Christ is in you, your body is dead because of sin, yet your spirit is alive because of righteousness. And if the Spirit of him who raised Jesus from the dead is living in you, will also give life to your mortal bodies through his Spirit who lives in you."

    The presence of the Spirit is evidenced by a Spirit-controlled life which in turn provide assurance that our resurrection is certain, even now.

3. Give us His spiritual gifts.
    1 Corinthians 12: 7–11 reads, "Now to each one the manifestation of the Spirit is given for the common good. To one there is given the message of wisdom, to

another the message of knowledge by means of the same Spirit, to another faith by the same Spirit, to another gifts of healing by that one Spirit, to another miraculous powers, to another prophecy, to another distinguishing between spirits, to another speaking in a different kinds of tongues and still to another the interpretation of tongues. All these are the work of the same Spirit and gives them to each one, just as he determines."

Every member of the body of Christ has been given a spiritual gift and that is evidenced by the Spirit working in his or her life. All the gifts are intended to build up the Christian community and not to be used for selfish advantage. Not everyone has the same gift nor all the gifts. The Holy Spirit sovereignly determines which gift or gifts each believer should have. For example, the spirit of wisdom may be given if there is a difficult decision to be made. The passage talks of different gifts (plural) of healing, which may refer to different ways of healing for different illnesses. It talks of miraculous powers – a miracle is an action that cannot be explained by natural means. It is an act of God intended to evidence His power and purpose. Prophecy is a communication of the mind of God imparted to the believer by the Holy Spirit. It can be a prediction or an indication of the will of God in a certain situation. The distinguishing of spirits is needed as there are false spirits. So we need to know if a prophecy is true or false. Speaking in tongues is an unlearnt human language. It is a communication of the mind of God imparted to a believer by the Holy Spirit. We are also encouraged to ask for the gifts, especially the gift of prophecy. I Corinthians 14 verse 1 reads, "Follow the way of love and eagerly desire spiritual gifts, especially the gift of prophecy."

4. Empower us to proclaim and heal.

The account of Peter and John at the temple gate is recorded in Acts 3:6–10. A beggar sitting at the temple gate had asked Peter and John for money.

Peter replied, "Silver and gold I do not have, but what I have I give to you. In the name of Jesus Christ of Nazareth, walk. Taking him by the right hand Peter helped him up and instantly the man's feet and ankles became strong. He jumped to his feet and began to walk. Then he went with them to the temple courts, walking and jumping and praising God." The people recognised him as the same man who used to sit begging at the temple gate called Beautiful and they were filled with wonder and amazement at what had happened to him.

This is an example how Jesus healed through Peter. It wasn't by Peter's power, but by the Holy Spirit flowing from Jesus.

This same power is available to believers today. I have seen many people healed of different ailments, serious and not so serious, including, my own son, whom the Lord healed of leukaemia.

When we lay hands on people and pray things happen. The Lord allows His Holy Spirit to flow through us to heal the person. In John 14:12 Jesus is speaking to his disciples. "I tell you the truth, anyone who has faith, in me will do what I have been doing. He will do even greater things than these, because I am going to the Father."

Jesus is saying miracles will happen because he was going to His Father. That was the purpose of the cross and then he would send us his Holy Spirit and His work would be done in the strength of the Holy Spirit.

Do we realise that we can have the seal of the Holy Spirit on our lives today?

TRUST

Key verse: Proverbs 3:5. "Trust in the Lord with all your heart, lean not on your own understanding."

When we talk about having trust in something or someone, it means we have a bold confidence and a sure security in them. When we are trusting God about a certain situation we have to wait for God's timing for it to come to fruition. We have to wait for his appointed time. This is always a faith building time. There may be no evidence that a sick person is improving, but we still have to trust God. We trust because of the faith we have and because we believe in the promises of God in all circumstances, even though the evidence seems contrary. Through trusting we get God's peace. Isaiah 26:3 says, "You will keep in perfect peace him whose mind is steadfast, because he trusts in you."

Our key verse encourages us to commit our ways to the Lord wholeheartedly and be ever mindful of the God we are serving. If we do this he will remove obstacles from our journey and bring us to our appointed goal. When we confess that we are trusting God it means we are believing in who He is and we must acknowledge Him in every part of our life. Trusting the Lord gives us an assurance that leads to action and it builds our faith, when serving the Lord. Confidence should infuse our whole being. The problem of relying on our understanding and trusting our discernments and knowledge is that our heart is deceitful. Jeremiah 17:9 says, "The heart is deceitful above all things." This is why we have to make sure we have denied ourselves and follow him. In Matthew 16:24 Jesus is recorded as saying, "If anyone would come after me, he must deny himself and take up his cross and follow me." This is a daily act so that our total trust is in Jesus.

When we become Christians we are given a new heart by Christ, through the Holy Spirit. We cultivate God-trusting hearts by meditating on scriptures, prayer and mixing with other Christians. In this way we can tune in to the Holy Spirit living within us and then we will rely less on ourselves and more on Christ. By acknowledging Him in all our ways, then whatever we are doing God is with us.

Jeremiah 17:7–8 records these words on trust, "But blessed is the man who trusts in the Lord, whose confidence is in Him. He will be like a tree planted by the water that sends out roots by the stream. It does not fear when heat comes its leaves are always green. It has no worries in a year of drought and never fails to bear fruit."

By trusting God we are giving all our anxieties and worries to Him and we can have peace even during troubled times.

Philippians 4:6,7 encourages us about not being anxious, "Do not be anxious about anything, but in everything, by prayer and petition, with thanksgiving, present your requests to God. And the peace of God, which transcends all understanding, will guard your hearts in Jesus Christ."

The benefit of trusting God is that we will have peace about our situations. Trusting the Lord is the only path to life. Jesus trusted His Father totally, even to His death and resurrection.

Only Jesus is unshakeable, unchangeable and unbreakable. Through Him is our salvation. God offers healing, wisdom and love to the world.

So acknowledge Him in all your ways.

We need to stand in awe of God and to live in respectful fear. Today we seem to have become very casual with God and lost that reverence and honour. To stand in awe of God or fear

God is not to be frightened, but to regard Him in high esteem, to obey Him and to acknowledge Him that He is worthy of honour as Creator and Judge. Deuteronomy 13:4 states, "It is the Lord your God you must follow and him you must revere. Keep his commands and obey him, serve him and hold fast to him."

It is so important to thank God for any slight improvement in a situation, however small it may seem. They are steps along the way to the ultimate goal. These steps will be faith-building and highlight our reliance on God. Zechariah 4:10 reminds us, "Do not despise the day of small beginnings." (*New Living Translation*).

God is calling us to a life of constant trust in Him. We need to learn to live above our circumstances. We need to talk to God about every aspect of our life. We need to ask the Holy Spirit to guide us, moment by moment, each day. In that way, we will keep close to God and truly trust Him.

Trust is an antidote to a troubled heart and a means to make sure that nothing comes between us and our relationship with God.

Totally

Rely

Upon our

Saviour's

Truth

USE (YOUR SENSES)

Key verse: Psalm34: 8. "Taste and see that the Lord is good."

God gave us five senses; sight, hearing, smell, taste and touch so that we could interact with the world around us. These five senses also enable us to interact with God.

SIGHT

With our eyes, it is so easy to see the beauty of the world around us and to see the faces of our families and friends. So often we take our sight for granted, how difficult to be blind and not have the use of this sense. Matthew 6:22 says, "The eyes are the lamp of the body. If your eyes are good your whole body will be full of light. But if your eyes are bad your whole body will be full of darkness." The eyes are the entrance to our hearts and a doorway to our souls. Not only do we see, but we perceive with our eyes. We form a judgement about things, good and evil. If we perceive goodness then our hearts will radiate that goodness and if we perceive evil our hearts will radiate despair. We guard our hearts and souls by guarding our eyes. As Christians, we should be seeing the world through God's eyes. The things He wants us to see and the path He wants us to take. So often we have blind spots in our vision and they have to be removed. Many people suffer from spiritual blindness and only see things from a human perspective. Even the Pharisees were spiritually blind. In Mark 8:16 we read of the Pharisees discussing amongst themselves in response to a comment made by Jesus. Apart from a single loaf the disciples had forgotten to bring bread. Jesus warns them to, "Watch out for the yeast of the Pharisees and that of Herod." Yeast was regarded as a symbol of evil or corruption and Jesus is warning the disciples to 'see' the true motives and intentions of the Pharisees. The Pharisees conclude that the comment made by Jesus relates to their being no bread to feed the assembled people. Jesus was talking to them on a spiritual level but they did not perceive what he was saying, as they still saw things on a human level. Two Corinthians 4:4 states, "The God of this age has blinded the minds of unbelievers so that they cannot see the light of the gospel of the glory of Christ, who is the image of God." The only way to cure spiritual blindness is to accept that Jesus is your Saviour and to have Him living in you by His Holy Spirit. It is as if a veil has been taken off our eyes so that we can see clearly. Isaiah 45: 22 expresses the exhortation to, "Turn to me and be saved." Then your eyes will be opened and you will see life from an eternal perspective as explained in 2 Corinthians 4:18, "So we fix our eyes not on what is seen but on what is unseen, for what is seen is temporary, but what is unseen is eternal."

HEARING

We need our sense of hearing all times, for we need to hear about the gospel of salvation. We need to hear from God what it is he wants us to do and to hear His hope for the future.

So often we are deaf in not hearing from God. We are told to incline our ears to the Lord. It is interesting that God gave us two ears but only one mouth! In Revelations, the phrase, "He who has an ear, let him hear," is often repeated at the end of the revelation to the seven churches. This gives a sense of not just hearing but paying close attention to what is being said, listening attentively. We have to be tuned in to God's Spirit. If we are not we will miss what he is saying and not be obedient to His call.

We need to hear this message of Hope from the Lord. In Hebrews 7:19 and 20 we read, "We have this hope as an anchor for our soul, firm and secure. It enters the inner sanctuary behind the curtain where Jesus, who went before us, has entered on our behalf." Just as a ship is anchored safely into position, our hope in Christ is guaranteed safety. As the ship's anchor goes down to the sea bed, the Christian's anchor goes up into the true heavenly sanctuary, where it is moored to God himself.

We have to learn the skill of listening. When Jesus appeared to Mary Magdalene after the crucifixion, she did not recognise Him. It wasn't until He said her name "Mary," did she realise it was the risen Lord. She knew the sound of His voice.

There is a difference between hearing and listening. Hearing is hearing the sound something makes, but listening means paying attention to and giving it consideration. God simply wants us to listen and the act of listening will lead to obedience. Sometimes, we may not recognise His voice at first. There is an amazing example of this in 1 Samuel 3:2–9. Samuel is under the care of the priest Eli.

"One night Eli, whose eyes were becoming so weak that he could barely see, was lying down in his usual place. The lamp of God had not yet gone out and Samuel was lying down in the temple of the Lord where the ark was. Then the Lord called Samuel. Samuel answered, "Here I am," and he ran to Eli and he said, "Here I am, you called me." But Eli said, "I did not call you; go back and lie down." So he went back and lay down. Again the Lord called, "Samuel" and Samuel got up and went to Eli and said, "Here I am, you called me." "My son," Eli said, "I did not call you; go back and lie down." Now Samuel did not yet know the Lord. The word of God had not been revealed to him. The Lord called Samuel a third time and Samuel got up and went to Eli and said, "Here I am, you called me." Then Eli realised that the Lord was calling the boy. So Eli told Samuel, "Go and lie down and if he calls you, say, "Speak Lord, for your servant is listening." So Samuel went and lay down in His place.

The Lord came and stood there, calling as at the other times, "Samuel, Samuel." Then Samuel said, "Speak, for your servant is listening."

Samuel heard a voice speaking to him but did not recognise it as the Lord's voice. Often we can worship God but do not know Him intimately. We should make ourselves available for God to speak. Quiet moments, such as the time when you go to bed provide an opportunity when like Samuel you can say, "Speak Lord for your servant is listening."'

Psalm 46:10 says, "Be still and know that I am God." We have to give God space to speak to us. He is longing to commune with us, but we are usually so busy that we end up shutting him out. We can build up our relationship with God through listening. Maybe we could review how long in a day we give Him the time to talk to us so we can listen.

SMELL

I expect there are aromas or fragrances that trigger different memories, some good, some bad. The smell of coffee brewing is often a pleasant aroma to many people, or the smell of the seaside evokes happy memories.

In Genesis 8:21 we read, "The Lord smelled the pleasing aroma." This was the Lord taking delight in Noah's worship to Him after he came out of the ark. In Ephesians 5:1,2 we read, "Be imitators of God, therefore, as dearly loved children and live a life of love just as Christ loved us and gave himself up to be a fragrant offering and sacrifice to God." This was extravagant love. As Jesus was a fragrant offering so we as followers are called to be a fragrant offering to others in the world. Two Corinthians 2:15 explains why this is important. "For we are the aroma of Christ among those who are being saved and those who are perishing." That means to some we are the smell of life, but to others the smell of death. We convey the aroma of Christ, to others, by our attitude our actions and our words.

We read in John Chapter 12 about Jesus being anointed by Mary with some very expensive perfume. In verse 3 of Chapter 12 it says, "Then Mary took about a pint of pure nard, an expensive perfume and poured it on Jesus's feet and wiped His feet with her hair. And the house was filled with the fragrance of the perfume." This act was showing Mary's love for Jesus and her humility. Jesus delighted in her worship of him. We need to worship Jesus in the same manner, so that our worship will be a fragrant offering to Him and one of thanksgiving and praise. We also need to be His fragrance to others we meet during our lives.

TASTE

Psalm 34:8 states, "O taste and see that the Lord is good."

In this scripture, God tells us to taste first and then see His goodness. So how do we do this? We read in Jeremiah 15:16, "When your words came I ate them; they were my heart's delight." He digested them and they became part of him. He so enjoyed them that he wanted to go back for more. It is the same when we try new foods, we taste a little bit and decide whether we like it, then if we do, we will go back for more. God doesn't just want us to know about Him, but He actually wants us to taste Him in our own hearts through His word. God's word carries the flavour of God which is sweet and good. If the word is tasteless to us, the problem isn't the word, but the way we approach it. We are reminded in Psalm 119:103–104, "How sweet are your words to my taste, sweeter than honey to my mouth. I gain understanding from your precepts." Just as we need food to sustain us physically, we also need spiritual food to sustain us spiritually.

Jesus made a strange statement in John 6:51, which the disciples didn't understand. He said, "I am the living bread that came down from Heaven. If anyone eats of this bread, he will live forever. This bread is my flesh, which I will give for the life of the world." If we read on into the following verses, 53–58, Jesus continues by saying, "I tell you the truth, unless you can eat the flesh of the Son of Man and drink his blood, you have no life in you. Whoever eats my flesh and drinks my blood has eternal life and I will raise him up on the last day. For my flesh is real food and my blood is real drink. Whoever eats my flesh and drinks my blood remains in me and I in him. Just as the living Father sent me and I live because of the Father, so the one who feeds on me will live because of me. This is the bread that came down from Heaven. Your forefathers ate manna and died, but he who feeds on this bread will live forever."

The truth that His body was broken for us and His blood spilled pays in full the penalty for our sin and that His perfect righteousness is freely given to us in exchange for our unrighteousness. Believing this is how we eat Jesus's flesh and drink His blood. The Lord's supper was instituted so that we would not forget our core belief.

TOUCH

There is something significant about the sense of a touch from someone. God's love can be experienced through this tangible gift. Jesus reached out with his healing touch to many people, lame, deaf and mute to name but a few. He also reached out and touched the untouchables. He actually touched lepers who were outcasts. In Matthew 8:1–3 we read, " When he came down from the mountainside large crowds followed him. A man with leprosy came and knelt before him and said, " Lord if you are willing, you can make me clean." Jesus reached out his hand and touched the man. 'I am willing.' He said, 'Be clean!'" Immediately he was cured of his leprosy. Jesus was willing to use his sense of touch to heal people. There is another example in Luke Chapter 17 where Jesus healed ten lepers. After they had been healed, only one came back to thank Jesus. He was praising God and fell at the feet of Jesus to thank Him. Jesus said to the one leper that returned, "Were not all ten lepers healed?" Yes, they were, but the nine who did not return only wanted to be healed, but the one that came back was actually seeking the healer and he received the extra blessing of his salvation.

It also happened the other way around, where those who were ill simply wanted to touch Jesus. We read, in Luke 8:43–48, about the woman with bleeding who was totally focussed on touching Jesus's cloak. When she touched the hem of his garment Jesus felt His power go out from him. Jesus said, "Who touched me?" Whenever you are touched by Jesus things change. She wanted to touch the healer himself. We often come near to Jesus to hear, but not near enough to be touched by Him. Everyone who came to Jesus was blessed. We need to surrender ourselves to Him so he can touch us. God touches our hearts with His Holy Spirit. This is personal and intimate. Romans 5:5 reminds us that, "God has poured out his love into our hearts by the Holy Spirit, whom he has given us."

There are moments in our lives when we know that God has touched us. These times are so precious, there is a sense of peace and holiness. We must treasure these times.

We are called as followers, to go out and lay hands on the sick so they can be healed. In Acts 28:8–10 we read about Paul visiting the house of Publicus, a chief official on the island of Malta. "His father was sick in bed, suffering from fever and dysentery. Paul went in to see him and, after prayer, placed his hands on him and healed him. After this had happened, the rest of the sick on the island came and were cured." The fact that one man, Paul, laid hands on this man had a ripple effect of others coming to him for healing.

We need to check whether we are engaging with all our five senses on our faith journey. Each one gives us important information about what is happening in our everyday and spiritual life. Our five senses empower us as followers of Jesus. Knowing God and witnessing for him requires all our five senses.

VEIL

Key verse: 2 Corinthians 3:16. "Whenever anyone turns to the Lord, the veil is taken away."

A veil is a covering that separates; a person outside of the veil does not know what, or who, is behind the veil. It is a mystery. There was a veil (curtain) in the temple that separated the Holy place from the Holy of Holies. Only the high priest was allowed into the Holy of Holies once a year for an hour. At the exact moment when Jesus died this curtain was torn in two.

Matthew 27:50,51 reads, "And when Jesus cried out again in a loud voice, he gave up his spirit. At that moment, the curtain of the temple was torn in two from top to bottom. The earth shook and the rocks split."

This meant the offering of the sacrifice of the lamb had been accepted by God. Here the promised Messiah had given himself to be the final sacrifice for sin. There was no more need for animal sacrifice. The barrier (veil) had now gone, so there was access for believers to God. As recorded in Hebrews Chapter 10 verses 19 and 20 we read, "Therefore, brothers, since we have confidence to enter the Most Holy Place by the blood of Jesus, by a new and living way opened for us through the curtain, that is, his body." Believers were able to come to the throne of Grace, since the perfect priest had offered the perfect sacrifice, atoning for sin once and for all. The tearing down of the curtain symbolises the body of Christ in his suffering. Like the curtain, his body was torn to open the way into the divine presence. This was a supernatural act by God.

This barrier which had been in the temple forever and ever, has now been removed. Behind the veil had been the Ark of the Covenant and that is where the Glory of the Lord was. In Hebrews 6:19 we read about the hope we have in Christ, as he is our anchor, "We have this hope as an anchor for the soul, firm and secure. It enters the inner sanctuary behind the curtain, where Jesus, who went before us, has entered on our behalf."

Before we become believers we all have a veil over our eyes. Satan has blinded people to truth so they cannot understand the purpose of God in Jesus. Unless this veil is removed no amount of study will result in a true understanding of the word. We need to fix our eyes on things beyond the veil. Not on the seen but the unseen. Not the visible material things we can actually see but the invisible, things of God and things above as they are eternal. As our key verse says, whenever anyone turns to Christ the veil is taken away. It is only in Christ that the veil can be removed. This is clearly stated in 2 Corinthians 3:14. "for to this day the same veil remains when the old covenant is read. It has not been removed because only in Christ is it taken away." This means that only by accepting Jesus's death and resurrection can the veil be removed and we can then receive the New Covenant in Christ.

If we are trying to serve God with our veil intact then we are blindsided. We are trying to hold on to the temporal things in the hope that they will last forever. We are missing great things from God. We need to turn to Jesus and ask Him to take away the veil that is preventing us from knowing Him. As the author of the book of Hebrews continues from our earlier quote from Chapter 10 we are encouraged to draw near to God (*verse 22*), but then the author lays down four conditions that will enable us to draw near to God, (*verses 22 and 23*);

These are;

1. A sincere heart, undivided allegiance.

2. Full assurance of faith, no hesitation in trusting and following Christ.

3. Hearts sprinkled to cleanse us from a guilty conscience, total freedom from a sense of guilt.

4. Having our bodies washed with pure water, inner cleansing.

He will take away the veil and we will see glorious eternal things.

We will see clearly the victory that Jesus has given the world. This victory though had to involve Jesus going through the agony of Gethsemane, where he cried out to his Father; "Father everything is possible for you. Take this cup from me. Yet not what I will, but what you will." (*Mark 14:36*). Jesus had total abandonment to the Father's will. We too have to be brought to that place of total abandonment. When we reach that point we know that our veil has been taken away.

I have always been fascinated by anagrams and altering letters around to make new words. I was looking at the word VEIL and thought there was a very simple message here. When the VEIL was torn down, a way was provided, for us to get rid of the EVIL and VILE things in our lives, so that we could LIVE the life God intended.

I pray this speaks to you too.

WISDOM

Key verse: James 1:5. "If any of you lacks wisdom,
he should ask God who gives generously to all without
finding fault and it will be given to him."

The dictionary definition of wisdom is:– 'the ability to think and act using knowledge, experience, understanding, common sense and insight.' Often we think that people who have a lot of knowledge are wise, but in truth they are often people who have just retained a lot of facts or information. People who have wisdom are the ones who have an understanding, a discernment and an insight into the facts.

The one gift we all need is God's wisdom to lead our lives on a daily basis. Today people seem unaware of sin and temptation. Anything goes, we accept things without question and we do what we want. We need wisdom not to be drawn into things that are not of God. The Devil is devious and will constantly try to trick us. We must pray for wisdom and discernment when we are not sure or when our spirit tells us to think again before we act or speak. In the book of James (*Chapter 3:13–16*), James describes two kinds of wisdom. The first is characterised by a good life, good deeds and actions done with the humility that comes from wisdom. The second is evidenced by bitter envy, selfish ambition and is described by James as earthly, unspiritual and of the devil. Wisdom is not just acquired information but practical insight with spiritual implications. When the Lord asked Solomon for anything he wanted, the one gift he asked for was wisdom. He could have asked for great wealth, riches or honour but he didn't.

Our key verse tells us that God's gift of wisdom is not only generous but given without finding fault. Further on in the book of James Chapter 3 and verse 17 we read, "But the wisdom that comes from heaven is first of all pure; then peace-loving, considerate, submissive, full of mercy and good fruit, impartial and sincere." There is a calmness about all these characteristics of God's wisdom and through them God will shine through. We need a pure heart that has been cleansed by the Holy Spirit, but through a heart that is muddled and full of deceitful things you will see everything but God. In Proverbs, we read that, "A heart at peace gives life to the body, but envy rots the bones." (*Proverbs 14:30*). Wise people will listen more and talk less and they will be sincere.

Proverbs 9:10 states, "The fear of the Lord is the beginning of wisdom." This means that you must have a loving reverence for God, which includes submission to his Lordship and to the commands of his word.

We live in a very untrusting and deceitful world and we need God's spiritual wisdom inside of us. There are so many decisions to be made every day. We need to see things from God's perspective in order to be wise about our decisions. It is necessary to change our perspective and ask ourselves, "How does God see my situation?" It is so easy to see only negatives when you are in a difficult situation and this can lead to a downward spiral of emotions and feelings. You can only see the problem from one perspective. There seems to be no way out. Perspective means how we perceive or view a situation. It is only the wisdom of God that can bring true counsel and insight. God can speak wisdom to us, through His Holy Spirit. It is wiser to walk in his ways as that will bring blessing and peace. "Counsel and sound judgment are mine; I have understanding and power." (*Proverbs 8:14*).

To be wise with God's wisdom is to be wise indeed. Often our intellectual pride can get in the way of hearing from God and get in the way of people receiving their salvation, which He desires to give. We think we know best! We need to humble ourselves before the Lord and seek His Counsel. If we ask Him for wisdom we must believe that He will give it and not doubt.

"But when he asks he must believe and not doubt, because he who doubts is like a wave of the sea, blown and tossed by the wind." (*James 1:6*).

The wisdom of God was displayed by Jesus throughout His life. The Holy Spirit wants to produce the same wisdom in all believers. When Jesus went into the desert after his baptism, the devil tried to tempt him, but each time God gave Jesus wisdom with his reply. Jesus dealt with each challenge from the devil with humility and wisdom. Another example of spiritual wisdom is when Paul prayed for the Colossian church. He wrote, "For this reason since the day we heard about you, we have not stopped praying for you, asking God to fill you with the knowledge of his will through all spiritual wisdom and understanding." (*Colossians 1:9*) If they have this wisdom then they will be living a life worthy of the Lord. Knowledge and wisdom are practical.

We need to realise that we live in a spiritual battle and the enemy lurks around the corner to trick us. As we read in Ephesians 6:12, "For our struggle is not against flesh and blood, but against the rulers, against the authorities, against the powers of this world and against the spiritual forces of evil in the heavenly realms." We all need God's wisdom to know how to deal with this and not be led astray. As recorded in Isaiah 48:17, "I am the Lord your God who teaches you what is best for you, who directs you in the way you should go."

Even the small decisions we make, we need to lay before the Lord. Sometimes we do not understand the wisdom of God we just need to obey it.

"For my thoughts are not your thoughts, neither are your ways, my ways declares the Lord. As the heavens are higher than the earth, so are my ways higher than yours ways and my thoughts than your thoughts." (*Isaiah 55:8,9*) Even man's greatest wisdom is only foolishness in God's sight.

To summarise:-

1. We need to tap into God's wisdom.

2. Diligently study God's Word.

3. Meditate on the Word (fully consider how to apply God's Word).

4. Pray for wisdom and seek it with all our heart and walk in the Spirit.

God's desire is to give His Wisdom to His children. Are you willing to receive it?

X-RAY

Key verse: 1 Samuel 16: 7b. "Man looks at the outward appearance, but the Lord looks at the heart."

I expect we have all had to have an X-ray at some point in our lives. The doctor has probably asked for this when there is something wrong with our body that he is unable to see. The machine is able to take a picture of bones or organs inside our body and then, after looking at the X-ray the doctor can decide the best course of action or treatment.

Some people look beautiful on the outside but inside are mean, selfish and hateful. Other people are not so beautiful on the outside, but on the inside are loving, kind and gentle. We often spend a lot of time, money and effort to look good on the outside but how long do we spend reflecting on how good we look on the inside? We can only see people from the outside but God sees us from the inside. When Samuel was looking for his successor, as recorded in 1 Samuel 16:7a, Samuel is considering Eliab, son of Jesse when the Lord says to him, "Do not consider his appearance or height, for I have rejected him." The Lord does not look at the things man looks at. Man looks at the outward appearance but the Lord looks at the heart.

We have a saying that you should not judge a book by its cover. What is written on the pages inside is the most important factor! Do you realise that God knows everything about us, the real me, my thoughts, my motives and all that I hold dear? As Luke writes in Chapter 11 and verse 39, "Then the Lord said to him (a Pharisee), Now then, you Pharisees clean the outside of the cup and dish, but inside you are full of greed and wickedness. You foolish people! Did not the one who made the outside make the inside also? But give what is inside the dish to the poor and everything will be clean for you." What comes from our heart is the real us. If you have no love in your heart you cannot give love.

I had a picture a few years ago of someone ironing. Before they ironed anything they turned the garments inside out so that they could iron the inside. They did this so that there would be no marks from the iron on the outside when they had finished. Once ironed, the person turned the garment the right way round and no marks or creases would be found. This is an illustration of what the Lord can do for us by his Holy Spirit. He irons out all the creases that are on our inside, in other words, all the wrong thoughts we are storing in our hearts. When He has finished we become as perfect as we can be and this results in the Holy Spirit radiating from us all the characteristics and qualities that the Lord wants the world to see.

Let us consider what these creases inside of us might be.

a. Wrong thoughts about someone.

b. Not doing what the Lord has shown us he wants us to do.

c. A broken relationship with someone, but we know we have to take the first step to heal it.

d. Not putting the Lord first, just doing what benefits us.

e. Not spending time in prayer.

The list is probably endless, but we each know deep down what the creases are in our own lives. So how do we iron out these creases in our lives?

First of all, we need to lay all these problems before the Lord. We are told to cast all our cares on Him because he cares for us. "Cast all your anxiety on him because he cares for you." (*1 Peter 5:7*).

Secondly, "Search me, O God and know my heart; test me and know my anxious thoughts. See if there is any offensive way in me and lead me in the way everlasting." (*Psalm 139:23,24*).

We need to allow the Holy Spirit to heal these wrong thoughts, as He brings them to the surface of our minds.

Everyone who has these problems or issues needs to be healed in their hearts. We have to be honest with ourselves. In James Chapter 5:16 it says, "Therefore confess your sins to each other and pray for each other, so that you may be healed. The prayer of a righteous man is powerful and effective." We need to get alongside wise Christians who will pray with us. If we continue to hold bitterness and malice in our hearts we actually grieve the Holy Spirit.

"Get rid of all bitterness rage and anger, brawling and slander, along with every form of malice. Be kind and compassionate to one another, forgiving each other, just as Christ God forgave you." (*Ephesians Chapter 4:31,32*).

We have to make room for Jesus in our hearts, so that all these worldly characteristics are removed from our hearts. They cannot co-exist. We are told in Romans Chapter 12:2, "Do not conform any longer to the pattern of this world, but be transformed by the renewing of your mind. Then you will be able to test and approve what God's will is – his good pleasing and perfect will." This is how we will grow and mature as Christians, as we allow the Holy Spirit to wash us clean. We have to allow His Life and His Love to permeate every part of our being. After being filled by His Holy Spirit we have to allow His Grace to be manifested in our lives.

So often we stop short of receiving all the blessings God has for us.

The Holy Spirit is our helper, whom Jesus promised to send. He will help us through every day. The disciples were told, by Jesus, to wait for the Holy Spirit to come. They had to wait as Jesus had not been glorified at that point. We, though, have the Holy Spirit here with us now, so we don't have to wait. The only waiting is on our part, depending on our spiritual fitness. Once Jesus was glorified in His ascension, then the Holy Spirit came into the world, and He has been here ever since. The receiving of the Holy Spirit into our lives should be a continued attitude from believers. We need a constant stream. The Holy Spirit is the evidence of the ascended Christ. We only have to ask the Lord for the Holy Spirit to come into our lives, we just receive it by God's grace.

So what would the heavenly X-ray, or even a scan say about each of us? Do I walk in repentance when the Lord puts his finger on something, or do I blame someone else and just excuse myself? So often we want all the benefits of the Kingdom but without the King.

Just want to end this section with three verses from Psalm 51:10–12, as a prayer for everyone.

"Create in me a pure heart, O God and renew a steadfast spirit within me. Do not cast me from your presence or take your Holy Spirit from me. Restore to me the joy of your salvation and grant me a willing spirit, to sustain me."

YES!

Key verse: 2 Corinthians 1:20. "For no matter how many promises God has made, they are 'Yes' in Christ. And so through him the 'Amen' is spoken by us to the glory of God."

There are thousands of promises of God, throughout the Bible. They are all waiting there to be received and claimed by us. Here is a list of just seven of these promises.

I will go with you.

I will protect you.

I will be your strength.

I will answer you.

I will provide for you.

I will give you power.

I will always love you.

I expect we have all made promises to different people, but most of them we have probably broken, or not carried through. With the promises of God, we know that He is faithful to all of his promises. Psalm 145:13 states that, "The Lord is faithful to all his promises and loving towards all he has made."

In other words, we can trust God with the promises he has made to us. He is unfailing and committed to us. His character never changes. "Jesus Christ is the same yesterday, today and forever." (*Hebrews 13:8*). Just back a couple of verses in Hebrews Chapter 13:5 we have the assurance that God will never leave us or forsake us. Once we have made a commitment to Him we have all these promises given to us. God also promises to complete what he has started in you. Philippians Chapter 1:6 says, "he who began a good work in you will carry it on to completion until the day of Jesus Christ."

As Christians we can stand on the promises of God and depend totally on Him as he is absolutely trustworthy.

You may have some of these following questions going round in your mind;–

Do you love me Lord? Answer, *YES*.

Will you forgive me Lord? Answer, *YES*.

Will you accept me Lord? Answer, *YES*.

Will you help me change Lord? Answer, *YES*.

Will you give me power to serve you Lord? Answer, *YES*.

Will you show me your Glory Lord? Answer, *YES*.

A few of the other promises of God are:–

i. We are accepted when we come to Jesus. "Whoever comes to me I will never drive away." (*John 6:37*)

ii. We are able to live life to the full. "I have come that they may have life and have it to the full." (*John 10:10*)

iii. We have friendship with Jesus. "You are my friends, if you do what I command." (*John 15:14*)

iv. We can have joy and peace. "As the Father has loved me, so have I loved you. Now remain in my love. If you obey my commands, you will remain in my love, just as I have obeyed my Father's commands and remain in his love. I have told you this so that my joy may be in you and that your joy may be complete." (*John 15: 9–11*)

Are you living in the fullest enjoyment of God's promises? Have you said 'Yes' to all his promises and claimed them for yourself? When you say yes to these promises you must believe and not doubt. We read in James Chapter 1: 6,7, "But when he asks he must believe and not doubt because he who doubts is like a wave of the sea tossed by the wind. That man should not think he will receive anything from the Lord, he is a double-minded man unstable in all he does." The Bible says do not be double-minded.

All the promises of God and all His blessings in heavenly places, are YES in Christ. Jesus is God's decisive YES to all believers.

Some people spend their whole life searching for Jesus but never really find Him. It is rather like the people who use a metal detector striving to find that piece of treasure. Heads are down with headphones on waiting for that telltale bleep that signifies the treasure may have been found. It occurred to me that the special treasure that is Jesus is freely available to everyone. Instead of looking down, we need to look up and seek his face. If we do that there will be a bleep in our heart- an awakening, an excitement. That is the point, we need to say, "Yes Lord, it is you, you are real, thank you."

The one amazing promise that we need to take hold of occurs in John Chapter 3:16, a very famous verse, it says, "For God so loved the world that he gave his one and only Son, that whoever believes in him shall not perish but have eternal life."

This is an amazing promise of God, that if we accept what Jesus has done for us, by dying on the cross and taking our place, then we are promised eternal life.

Have you said "Yes?"

ZOOM

Key verse: James 4: 8. "Come near to God and He will come near to you."

There are different meanings to the word zoom. It can refer to the very fast movement of something and it can also refer to a camera moving in for a close-up. Today people are more familiar with the word zoom referring to a brand name for computer software. Families have been able to meet friends and families on Zoom calls and also businesses are able to have meetings.

The meaning I would like to focus on is the second one, where a camera can increase the magnification of a distant object by a zoom lens. I think this is very apt as an end to my tour of a biblical alphabet, as it is something we all need to do as Christians. We need to magnify our image of God and His character.

Most people prefer a beautiful view from a distance rather than a close-up of something. So often we settle for the beautiful view and not the close-up which will enrich us so much. God wants that intimate relationship with each of us and we have to draw near to Him to have that. We need to take the first step and put our zoom lens on. A zoom lens allows us to get closer, but at the same time, it keeps the picture in focus. We take the first step and then adjust the focus.

"Let us draw near to God with a sincere heart in full assurance of faith, having our hearts sprinkled to cleanse us from a guilty conscience and our bodies washed with pure water. Let us hold unswervingly to the hope we profess for He who promised is faithful" (*Hebrews 10:22,23*)

When you get a close-up of someone you can see the small details that you can't see from a distance. It is not that God has moved away from us, but that we have moved away from Him. He is constantly and patiently waiting for us to come closer to Him, "Come near to God and He will come near to you." (*James 4:8*). As we draw nearer to Him He reciprocates. That is a guarantee.

So how do we draw near to God? First of all, we need to make the decision that we want to draw near to Him and have a deeper relationship with Him. We need to come with a humble heart, in submission to His will, to glorify Him. God is looking for a sincere heart, confident faith and a clean conscience. It is an invitation from God. We need to spend time with him in prayer, listening and receiving from Him. Praise and worship help us to express our love for Him. We can be lost in His presence. We need to be in tune with God to know His will and plans for our lives.

"For I know the plans I have for you, declares the Lord, plans to prosper you and not to harm you, plans to give you hope and a future. Then you will call upon me and I will listen to you." (*Jeremiah 29:11,12*)

Why would we want to draw nearer to God? Firstly God want us to. Blessings will result when we do. He will be with us continually as we walk through life. He takes hold of our hand just as a loving father would with his son or daughter.

"For I am the Lord, your God, who takes hold of your right hand and says to you. Do not fear, I will help you." (*Isaiah 41:13*).

We have to move further away from worldliness, although the enemy will always try to draw us back. We will be tempted and distracted, but as we enlarge our perspective of God and continue in a relationship with Him, nothing will entice us away, it will only deepen our faith and trust in our Lord.

"Submit yourselves, then, to God. Resist the devil and he will flee from you. Come near to God and He will come near to you." (*James 4:7*).

As we spend more time with God, reading our Bibles, its words are a lamp to our feet and with other Christians we will cultivate the fruit of the Spirit. "But the fruit of the Spirit is love, joy, peace, patience, kindness, goodness, faithfulness, gentleness and self-control." (*Galatians 5:22,23*)

God wants us to enlarge our spiritual eyes so we can enlarge our capacity for joy. We need to adjust our spiritual lens. So often we walk through life with our eyes looking at the ground. We need to lift our heads to seek the Lord.

God has done everything necessary so we can come close to Him and rest in his presence. He gave us His Spirit to live inside of us so that we could live with Him every moment of our lives.

We also must come with a thankful heart to God and be obedient to His voice.

"Enter His gates with thanksgiving and His courts with praise; give thanks to Him and praise His name." (*Psalm 100:4*).

We need to praise Him for even the smallest of blessings. So often we want God to bless us with something huge and totally amazing, but each day there are things that God blesses us with. When you wake up in the morning it means that God has given you another day. Thank Him. Do we have a roof over our heads? Thank Him. Do we have food? Thank Him. Are we able to see or smell his beautiful creation? Thank Him. The list is endless.

We are told "Delight yourself in the Lord and He will give you the desires of your heart."(*Psalm 37:4*)

We have to consciously make that decision. The Lord has to be the desire of our hearts. He is the anchor of our soul.

There are many scriptures that say, "Come to me." We have to cease resisting the magnetic pull of His love. So often we can explain the vastness of His love for us, but we need to experience it.

"I pray that out of his glorious riches he may strengthen you with power through His Spirit in your inner being, so that Christ may dwell in your hearts through faith. And I pray that you, being rooted and established in love, may have power, together with all the saints, to grasp how wide and long and high and deep is the love of Christ and to know this love that surpasses knowledge – that you may be filled to the measure of all the fulness of God." (*Ephesians 3:16–19*).

The first verse here talks about our inner being and being strengthened by His power. It is the Holy Spirit that gives us this power. It is from the inner being (the soul) that all our decisions are made. Our abundance of power comes from the abundance of your spiritual wealth. Paul prays here that the believers will have the spiritual power that flows from His vast, limitless resources. We need to experience the full benefit of our relationship with the Lord. So often we are spiritual paupers.

How deep are your spiritual roots? As the roots of a tree keep it strong and stable, so our spiritual roots will give us a firm foundation in our faith. As tree roots go deeper and deeper in search of nutrients, so it is with us as we go deeper and deeper, spiritually, the love of Christ will nourish and stabilise us. There is an endless supply. To have a solid spiritual base, we need to have a relationship with Jesus.

As you zoom in to get closer to God, how big is He to you? Many years ago there was a song that was very popular with children at church, as it had actions all the way through. It was:–

My God is so big, so strong and so mighty,

There's nothing my God cannot do.

My God is so big, so strong and so mighty,

There's nothing that He cannot do.

The rivers are his, the mountains are his.

The stars are his handiwork too.

My God is so big, so strong and so mighty.

There's nothing that he cannot do.

My God is so big, so strong and so mighty,

There's nothing that he cannot do.

My God is so big, so strong and so mighty,

There's nothing that he cannot do.

He's called you to live for him every day,

In all that you say and you do.

My God is so big, so strong and so mighty,

There's nothing that he cannot do. *(Kenneth Morris)*

I think this song just sums up the omnipotence, omniscience and omnipresence of our God. Is this your God? Do you believe the words of this song or are you limiting what God can do? We need to magnify our Lord and make Him a bigger part of our lives. Mary, on hearing that she was to bear the child Jesus exclaimed in words now recorded in the Magnificat. "My soul doth magnify the Lord."

I would like to finish with a verse from Ephesians Chapter 3 verses 20 and 21. *(KJV)* "Now to him who is able to do exceedingly, abundantly above all that we ask or think, according to the power that worketh in us, unto him be glory in the church by Christ Jesus throughout all ages, world without end. Amen"

CONCLUSION

I pray that this little book has inspired you to feed on the promises of God. If we fuel our hearts and minds with His amazing promises, it will help us through life whatever circumstances we have to endure. Build your life on these promises. My desire is that you find these promises of God and feed on them throughout your life.

Milton Keynes UK
Ingram Content Group UK Ltd.
UKHW030713041024
449263UK00001B/84

9 781803 819938